Pascale Couture

482   597   225 +
                209 +
westin   209

   1 613 560 7000

Les Fougeres - rest.
#5 route 10 mins W.
exit B bear right
at T junction turn right
            on the right.

ULYSSES
TRAVEL PUBLICATIONS
Travel better... enjoy more

Editorial *Series Director:* Claude Morneau; *Project Supervisor:* Pascale Couture.

Research and Composition *Author:* Pascale Couture.

Production *Design:* Patrick Farei (Atoll Direction); *Proofreading:* Tara Salman, Sarah Kresh; *Translation:* Tracy Kendrick, Danielle Gauthier, Sarah Kresh; *Cartography:* André Duchesne, Patrick Thivierge (Assistant); *Graphics:* Isabelle Lalonde; *Layout:* Stéphane G. Marceau.

Illustrations *Cover Photo:* David Flaconer (Superstock); *Chapter Headings:* Jennifer McMorran; *Drawings:* Lorette Pierson.

Special Thanks to Benoit Prieur; Lorette Pierson; Benoit Éthier; François Rémillard; SODEC and the Department of Canadian Heritage for their financial support.

Distributors

AUSTRALIA:
Little Hills Press
11/37-43 Alexander St.
Crows Nest NSW 2065
☎ (612) 437-6995
Fax: (612) 438-5762

BELGIUM AND
LUXEMBOURG:
Vander
Vrijwilligerlaan 321
B-1150 Brussel
☎ (2) 762 98 04
Fax: (2) 762 06 62

CANADA:
Ulysses Books & Maps
4176 Saint-Denis
Montréal, Québec
H2W 2M5
☎ (514) 843-9882,
ext.2232
or 1-800-748-9171
Fax: 514-843-9448
www.ulysses.ca

GERMANY AND AUSTRIA:
Brettschneider
Fernreisebedarf
Feldfirchner Strasse 2
D-85551 Heimstetten
München
☎ 89-99 02 03 30
Fax: 89-99 02 03 31

GREAT BRITAIN AND
IRELAND:
World Leisure Marketing
9 Downing Road
West Meadows, Derby
UK DE21 6HA
☎ 1 332 34 33 32
Fax: 1 332 34 04 64

ITALY:
Centro Cartografico del
Riccio
Via di Soffiano 164/A
50143 Firenze
☎ (055) 71 33 33
Fax: (055) 71 63 50

NETHERLANDS:
Nilsson & Lamm
Pampuslaan 212-214
1380 AD Weesp (NL)
☎ 0294-465044
Fax: 0294-415054
E-mail: nilam@euronet.nl

PORTUGAL:
Dinapress
Lg. Dr. Antonio de Sousa
de Macedo, 2
Lisboa 1200
☎ (1) 395 52 70
Fax: (1) 395 03 90

SCANDINAVIA:
Scanvik
Esplanaden 8B
1263 Copenhagen K
DK
☎ (45) 33.12.77.66
Fax: (45) 33.91.28.82

SPAIN:
Altaïr
Balmes 69
E-08007 Barcelona
☎ 454 29 66
Fax: 451 25 59
E-mail:
altair@globalcom.es

SWITZERLAND:
OLF
P.O. Box 1061
CH-1701 Fribourg
☎ (026) 467.51.11
Fax: (026) 467.54.66

U.S.A.:
The Globe Pequot Press
6 Business Park Road
P.O. Box 833
Old Saybrook, CT 06475
☎ 1-800-243-0495
Fax: 1-800-820-2329
E-mail:
sales@globe-pequot.com

Other countries, contact Ulysses Books & Maps (Montréal), Fax: (514) 843-9448

"Grandeur is written on thy throne,
Beauty encompasseth thy mien;
The glory of the North alone,
Is thine, O Ottawa, my Queen."

James E. Caldwell,
"Ottawa", 1907.

TABLE OF CONTENTS

LIST OF MAPS

Canadian Cataloguing in Publication Data
Couture, Pascale, 1966-
    Ottawa
    (Ulysses travel guides)
    Translation of: Ottawa
    Includes index.
    ISBN 2-89464-170-2
1. Ottawa (Ont.) - Guidebooks. 2. Ottawa Region (Ont.) - Guidebooks.
 I. Title. II. Series.
FC3096.18.C7713 1998   917.13'84044   C98-940812-4
F1059.5.O9C7713 1998

Help make Ulysses Travel Guides even better!

The information contained in this guide was correct at press time.
However, mistakes can slip in, omissions are always possible, places
can disappear, etc. The authors and publisher hereby disclaim any
liability for loss or damage resulting from omissions or errors.

We value your comments, corrections and suggestions, as they allow
us to keep each guide up to date. The best contributions will be
rewarded with a free book from Ulysses Travel Publications. All you
have to do is write us at the following address and indicate which
title you would be interested in receiving (see the list at the end of
guide).

Ulysses Travel Publications
4176 Rue Saint-Denis
Montréal, Québec
Canada H2W 2M5
www.ulysse.ca
e-mail: guiduly@ulysse.ca

TABLE OF SYMBOLS

🛥	Ulysses' favourite
☎	Telephone number
⇌	Fax number
≡	Air conditioning
⊗	Ceiling fan
♿	Wheelchair access
🐩	Pets allowed
≈	Pool
ℜ	Restaurant
⊛	Whirlpool
ℝ	Refrigerator
K	Kitchenette
△	Sauna
⊙	Exercise room
sb	Shared bathroom
½b	half-board (lodging + 2 meals)
bkfst	Breakfast

ATTRACTION CLASSIFICATION

★	Interesting
★★	Worth a visit
★★★	Not to be missed

HOTEL CLASSIFICATION

Unless otherwise indicated, the prices in the guide
are for one room in the high season,
double occupancy, not including taxes.

RESTAURANT CLASSIFICATION

$	$10 or less
$$	$10 to $20
$$$	$20 to $30
$$$$	$30 or more

Unless otherwise indicated, the prices in the guide are for a
meal for one person, including taxes, but not drinks and tip.

All prices in this guide are in Canadian dollars.

Where is Ottawa ?

ONTARIO
Capital: Toronto
Population: 10,753,573 inhab.
Area: 1,068,630 km²

OTTAWA
Population: 324,000 inhab.
Area: 5138 km²

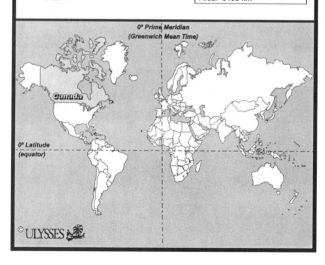

© ULYSSES

PORTRAIT

European explorers were first drawn to this area because of its location on the banks of the Ottawa River near the Chaudière Falls. Later, this site, surrounded by a seemingly infinite forest, was deemed strategic to British authorities, who decided to dig a canal and build a village here. In less than 200 years, this tiny hamlet metamorphosed into a beautiful national capital. Strolling along its streets, you can see for yourself just how lovely a city Ottawa has become, with its splendid Victorian buildings, vast green spaces and outstanding museums, that boast some of the finest collections in the country.

GEOGRAPHY

When Europeans began exploring Canada, the Ottawa River immediately became one of the major means of access into the territory. It was not, however, the easiest route, for it was studded with all sorts of natural obstacles, including the Chaudière Falls. It was at the foot of these falls that two towns sprouted up – first Wrightown (Hull), on the north shore, then Bytown (Ottawa), on the south shore, at the mouth of the Rideau River, at the eastern extremity of what is now the province of Ontario.

These two towns were set in the midst of a dense, boreal forest made up of evergreens like pine, spruce and fir, as well as a smaller number of deciduous species, such as aspen, birch and willow. The acidity of the soil made the land ill-suited to farming, so early settlers gradually gave up on agriculture and turned to the forest for their livelihood. Over the years, the lumber industry flourished, causing the forest to shrink dramatically. However, thanks to the creation of Gatineau National Park (Québec), a vast expanse of woodland has survived untouched.

POPULATION

Ottawa evolved from a tiny village in the heart of a dense forest to a proud and beautiful capital city within the space of a century. Today, it covers an area of 5,138 square kilometres and has 324,000 inhabitants (nearly a million including the suburban population). Greater Ottawa includes both Ontario towns, such as Vanier and Kanata, and Québec towns, such as Hull, Aylmer and Gatineau.

The majority of Ottawa residents are Anglophone (46.8%), Francophone (9.6%) or people who consider themselves bilingual (42.6%), meaning they speak both French and English. Among this majority, 57% are Catholic and 27% Protestant. Canadians of neither French nor British descent account for 15% of the population.

HISTORY

Ottawa did not spring into being spontaneously. In fact, it was founded fairly late (1825) in response to military and political imperatives, unlike older cities such as Montréal and New York, born of commerce. Ottawa owes its existence to the events that took place when Europeans first started colonizing Canada.

Colonization

Officially, John Cabot was the first European to reach the shores of Canada, in 1497. He was followed by Jacques

Cartier, in 1534 and on two other voyages. In search of a route to Asia, Cartier sailed along the coast of Labrador and up the St. Lawrence River to a native settlement named Hochelaga, located on the site now occupied by Montréal. There was no real follow-up to these voyages, however. In fact, it wasn't until the early 17th century that France started taking an interest in Canada again, due to the rage for fur clothing in Europe. Little by little, permanent trading posts were established on the Atlantic coast and inland in order to strengthen ties with local suppliers. In 1605, Port-Royal, in Acadia, was built; then, in 1608, Champlain and his men founded Québec City, which started out as a handful of fortified buildings. A permanent French presence was thus established in North America.

In the early years of colonization, French activity in North America centred mainly around the fur trade. A few missionaries, determined to convert the natives to Christianity, also made their way across the ocean. At the same time, the French slowly began to populate the territory. In 1663, when New France became a French province, it only had 3,000 inhabitants.

New France reached its apogee at the dawn of the 18th century, when it had a monopoly on the fur trade in North America and controlled the St. Lawrence River. However, in 1713, after being defeated in Europe, the French handed over control of Hudson Bay and Acadia to the English, who thus obtained part of the fur trade and a number of strategic military posts. In 1763, four years after Québec City was conquered by the British, France ceded New France to England under the Treaty of Paris. At the time, the territory was inhabited by some 60,000 French colonists.

In the years following the British Conquest, the Canadian population was still largely French. The territory west of the Ottawa River remained virtually unsettled, occupied only by native bands and fur traders. At that time, the British Crown had no plans to colonize or develop the territory beyond expanding the fur trade.

The American Revolution (1775-1783), however, led to the founding of Ontario and radically changed the history of Canada. In the first few years of this war between Great Britain and her 13 colonies in southern North America, British troops scouted out strategic positions in Ontario from which to launch attacks on the American rebels. Overall, however, the British and their allies found themselves at a disadvantage, and finally had to accept defeat. The American Revolution, at the beginning at least, was a true civil war pitting supporters of American independence against Loyalists wishing to maintain colonial ties with Great Britain. Over 350,000 of the latter fought alongside the British in the war. In 1783, the signing of the Treaty of Versailles, which recognized Great Britain's defeat at the hands of the American revolutionaries, prompted tens of thousands of Loyalists to take refuge in Canada. Between 5,000 and 6,000 moved to the virgin lands of the west, now Ontario, founding the first permanent colonies in that region. Most, however, settled along the north shore of the St. Lawrence River and Lake Ontario.

In 1791, London promulgated the Constitutional Act, which divided Canada into two provinces, Lower Canada and Upper Canada. Lower Canada, which included the territory settled by the French, remained subject to French civil law, while Upper Canada, located west of the Ottawa River and populated mainly by former Loyalists, was subject to English common law.

Bytown

In the years following the American Revolution, the colonists of Upper Canada regarded their neighbours to the south with distrust, and with good reason. In 1812, claiming to be tired of Britain's strict control over the Great Lakes, the Americans declared war on that country and, consequently, on Canada. The Loyalists and their descendants still constituted the bulk of the population of Upper Canada, so emotions ran high. Great Britain, busy with the Napoleonic Wars in Europe, was unable to offer its colony much help. The settlers nonetheless managed to fend off the American attack, causing the United States to suffer the first military defeat in its brief history.

Though invasion had been narrowly avoided, this war illustrated how isolated Upper Canada was geographically. The rapids that hindered travel up the St. Lawrence River in many places made the colony vulnerable in times of war and limited trade in times of peace. To improve the situation, canals were dug in several places along the St. Lawrence, notably in Lachine (1814) and Welland (1824).

Fear of a new conflict with the Americans also prompted British authorities to dig a third canal, the Rideau Canal, linking the Ottawa River to Fort Henry (Kingston). Not everyone approved of this project, however; the governments of Upper and Lower Canada, preoccupied with the construction of the Welland and Lachine Canals, were not in favour of colossal sums being spent on digging a new waterway. They were opposed by the British government, which considered the Rideau Canal to be a military necessity. In 1825, abandoning all hope of obtaining any financial contribution from the two other governments, the British began construction.

Back in 1823, Governor Dalhousie had purchased 160 hectares of land for the British Crown on the south shore of the Ottawa River, opposite Wrightown (present-day Hull), a small farming community founded by Philemon Wright in 1800. It was here that construction began on the canal in 1826, under the supervision of Lieutenant-Colonel By. A small village developed, inhabited by labourers who had come to dig the canal and officials sent to oversee the project. It was named Bytown after the Lieutenant-Colonel.

The British government, which owned a good portion of the land around the canal, also charged Governor Dalhousie and Lieutenant-Colonel By with developing the territory, and policies encouraging settlers to the region were adopted. These policies reflected the values of the two men: affluent English officials interested in leasing property were offered excellent terms and awarded the best lands, those west of the canal, which became Upper Town. A few shopkeepers, workers and lumberjacks, mainly French-speaking or Irish Catholics, took up residence on the east shore of the canal, where the land, though not as desirable, had been drained in 1827, creating Lower Town. These two groups had radically different points of views and rarely agreed on anything, so the development of the town was accompanied by much dissension.

It was impossible to oppose this arrangement, since there were only three landowners: the British government and two individuals. Nicholas Sparks owned about 80 hectares – a good portion of Upper Town – which afforded him a substantial income, while Louis Besserer owned land on the east bank of the canal, which he later subdivided.

Bytown 1830-1850

In Bytown's early years, authorities viewed agriculture as the key to the region's economic development. However, due to the local climate and geology (the acidic soil of the boreal forest), harvests were not as abundant as expected. In fact, the land was ill-suited to agriculture. Gradually, local residents gave up on farming and turned to the forest, which seemed like another possible source of income.

The canal, completed in 1832, did not serve its intended purpose either. Yes, it was a new waterway, but it definitely would not be as useful as hoped. Its large number of locks made it a slow and expensive route. The cost was that much higher because the merchants of Montréal and Kingston set the lock fees as they pleased. Furthermore, since there were no more conflicts between Canada and the United States, the canal never served its primary, military function.

It was thus the forest that enabled Bytown to attain a certain level of prosperity. Many residents became lumberjacks, either as their sole source of income or to offset poor harvests. Though many people earned their living cutting down trees, it was the transportation of the logs that truly enabled the town to flourish. Once chopped down, the trees were floated to Montréal on the Ottawa River. En route, the raftsmen (*draveurs* in French) had to confront a sizable obstacle: the Chaudière Falls, on the outskirts of Bytown. Since they had no choice but to stop and take apart their rafts, they would take the opportunity to stock up on supplies at the same time. Many businesses sprang up to meet their needs. In 1841, Bytown had 3,000 inhabitants at the most but no fewer than 38 shops; within four years, that number had risen to 51.

Though the lumber industry enabled many residents to earn a living, it did not provide much economic stability, as prices fluctuated according to demand. A drop in the price of wood, such as occurred in 1846, inevitably caused a depression in Bytown, prompting many people to leave. In short, the lumber industry enabled many people to survive but made few rich.

The vulnerable local economy, combined with the long-term lease policies established by the administration, also affected Bytown's appearance. In the 1850s, nothing was really built to last, aside from a few government buildings and a handful of large, opulent residences in Upper Town. The town was essentially a collection of flimsy little wooden houses. Furthermore, it was not developing around a single centre of activity, but rather in two parts, Upper Town and Lower Town, which seemed to be constantly at odds with one another.

This opposition was a source of tension, particularly between the various religious groups, namely the Catholics, who made up 58% of the population of Bytown and lived in Lower Town, and the Protestant minority who lived in Upper Town and were supported by area farmers. Conflicts also existed within the Catholic community, which was not a homogenous group. Irish and French descendents, who were frequently competing for the same jobs, often had violent altercations. The source of this rivalry lay in each individual's desire to improve his or her own lot. In the early 1850s, Bytown had only a few thousand inhabitants, who were too concerned with survival to envision the unusual fate that awaited their town.

From Small Town to Capital

In 1840, the colonies of Lower and Upper Canada were joined under the Act of Union. The following year, Kingston, a small military garrison that had become a bustling town thanks to the canalization of the St. Lawrence River, was chosen to be the seat of Parliament. Not everyone was pleased with this choice, however. Toronto, Montréal and Québec all felt slighted. Furthermore, Kingston's proximity to the United States and the never-ending fear of an American invasion put the British government ill at ease. Parliament was moved to Montréal two years later, then back to Kingston in 1849. The time had clearly come to settle on one safe place to establish the government.

Bytown was also examining its options during this period, with many local residents looking for ways to promote its growth. The arrival of the railroad, which revolutionized the transportation of merchandise, gave them hope that their town would become a regional railway hub. It didn't take them long to figure out that this was not going to happen, since Bytown was not located on the communication route between Montréal and Toronto. Efforts were made, however, to link the town to the American market by laying out a railway line between Bytown and Prescott. Unfortunately, this inefficient line took years to build and gobbled up a fortune in the process.

The Chaudière Falls offered a better means of sprucing up the local economy. Toward the 1850s, sawmills were built at the foot of the falls, but it wasn't until 1853 that the Crown, which owned Victoria Island, started selling off plots of land for the construction of mills that truly capitalized on the falls' potential as a source of energy. The sale of these lands enabled entrepreneurs like Harris and Bronson to build a mill. Blasdell, Currier and Co., which owned a mill at the foot of the falls, took the opportunity to increase their capacity. Finally, a third player came on the scene: Philip Thompson, who built saw-, flour, oat and carding mills, as well as a spinning mill on Chaudière Island. Even though ownership of these mills soon passed into the hands of rich American businessmen, who invested the major part of their profits in their own country, Bytown still enjoyed a definite economic boost.

While the economy of Bytown was taking shape, the powers that ruled United Canada were focussing their efforts on finding the perfect location for their capital. Though Montréal, Toronto, Kingston and Québec City were all vying for the honour, Bytown appealed to many people. In fact, though some saw it as a drab, violent place, it had a lot to recommend it: it was at the border of what used to be Upper and Lower Canada; it had an equal number of French- and English-speaking residents, and the British government owned pieces of land there that would provide perfect sites for government buildings. For these reasons, and also because the choice was less controversial politically, Macdonald and Cartier's Liberal-Conservative party favoured Bytown. To get their way, these two men demanded that the decision be made by the executive branch of the government; it is highly unlikely that this poor little town would have become the capital of United Canada if democracy had

The Odawa

Ottawa was named after the Algonquian tribe that used to live in the Ottawa Valley. The name apparently means "to trade". These First Nation people lived on farming, hunting, fishing and trade, and used the Ottawa River as a route inland. Their economy, closely linked to those of other tribes such as the Huron, who lived on the shores of Georgian Bay, was greatly disrupted by the arrival of the first Europeans. When the Iroquois destroyed Huronia in 1649, the Odawa were forced to flee westward. They didn't return to Ontario until about 20 years later, when they settled on Manitoulin Island and around the Great Lakes.

come into play. In 1857, Bytown, renamed Ottawa, officially became the capital.

The Development of Ottawa

Ottawa residents could not have hoped for more. Colossal sums were immediately allotted for the Parliament Buildings. Construction began in 1859, creating an employment boom and thus attracting scores of workers and merchants to the area. Though the project did not always go smoothly, Parliament was able to hold its first session in 1866 in a partially finished building. The following year, the Dominion of Canada was created. Originally, this confederation was made up of four provinces: New Brunswick, Nova Scotia, Québec (formerly Lower Canada) and Ontario (formerly Upper Canada). One day, however, the Dominion of Canada would stretch from the Atlantic to the Pacific, with Ottawa as its capital.

The splendid neo-Gothic buildings that house the Parliament and the city's major government institutions dominated Ottawa's urban landscape, along with the steeples of the various local churches. However, a number of neighbourhoods were in a pitiful state; wooden houses were often destroyed by fire, the dirt roads became unrideable during the spring thaw, the drainage system was inadequate, and sanitary conditions needed to be improved throughout the city. A lot of work needed to be done.

The city began to undergo a transformation in the late 1860s, when it became clear that its drainage system had to be modernized. However, it was only after a clear assessment of what exactly the city required and a lengthy evaluation of all possible solutions that construction was finally begun in the late 1870s. This new drainage system also led to the creation of an efficient fire brigade. Electricity, which started to become available in Ottawa around 1885, also helped shape the capital's new face, as certain streets, notably Sparks and Sussex, were equipped with streetlamps, and streetcars gradually replaced horse-drawn vehicles. Finally, a police force was set up to keep a curb on violence.

Another aspect of Ottawa's transformation in the second half of the 19th century was its expansion; several parts of town, like Lebreton, an industrial sector by the Chaudière Falls, and Lower Town, grew considerably. This expansion was partly the result of the government's decision to start selling land in the 1850s. New parts of town were also developed. Louis Besserer's land in the area known as Sandy Hill was subdivided so that elegant new houses could be built there.

All these changes, combined with new employment opportunities, attracted scores of newcomers, and the population of the city more than doubled at the end of the 19th century. This metamorphosis did not, however, alter the social fabric, which still contained great rifts. Lower Town, gradually abandoned by the Irish community in favour of other parts of Ottawa, became a bastion of Francophone culture, prompting French-speakers to take action to protect their rights, particularly the right to be educated in French. Over the years, however, the power of the Francophones was eclipsed by that of the wealthy Anglophone communities of Upper Town, whose members had many of the most prestigious and best-paying jobs in town. Furthermore, the Anglophone community never seemed to stop growing. Another area, Sandy Hill, expanded rapidly and also came to play a prominent role in the city's evolution. It was different from the other two neighbourhoods in that it was home to Catholics and Protestants of all different origins. Most residents belonged to a new group: the city's well-to-do political elite.

PORTRAIT

The 20th Century and Modernity

At the dawn of the 20th century, Ottawa's fate seemed extremely promising, since it was closely linked to that of Canada, which was entering a period of tremendous economic growth at the time. The Nation's optimistic prime minister, Sir Wilfrid Laurier, predicted that the 20th century belonged to Canada, and therefore, to Ottawa. Laurier was convinced that Ottawa was destined for a brilliant future, thanks to the growth of its paper and manufacturing industries. He also reintroduced the idea of digging a canal between Ottawa and Georgian Bay.

Laurier's hopes soon faded once it became evident that local industries could only expand so much. Be that as it may, Ottawa, whose civil service was constantly growing, continued to bustle with activity.

Ottawa's expansion also involved a substantial increase in the local population, which passed the 110,000 mark during World War I. Given the city's now considerable size, authorities were forced to tackle various issues related to urbanization and public health, with water treatment and health care facilities at the top of the list.

From 1929 to 1945, Canada's economic, political and social structure were severely disrupted by two international events, the economic crisis and World War II. The Great Depression of the 1930s halted Canada's economic growth. In Ottawa, as everywhere else in the country, a large portion of the population became unemployed. The government offered little assistance, and the jobless were left to fend for themselves. Poverty set in. The problem was so serious that in 1933 an unemployment programme administered by the Public Welfare Department had to be set up, thus heralding the creation of the welfare state.

World War II led to an explosion in the number of civil servants in Ottawa, which increased from 12,000 (1939) to 36,000 (1945) in the space of six years. Later, as the Canadian government adopted a more and more interventionist stance domestically, the civil service continued to grow, reaching its peak in the 1970s.

With the expansion of the federal government and the resulting increase in the number of civil servants, the city grew at lightning speed. There was a construction boom (government buildings, big commercial buildings, housing developments, etc.), which transformed certain neighbourhoods and pushed the city limits ever outwards. The city's layout, which authorities had futilely attempted to redesign at various times during the first half of 20th century, started to take a definite shape in the 1960s. Since then, the city has been in a state of constant improvement.

POLITICS

The British North America Act of 1867, the constitutional document that forms the basis of Canadian Confederation, divides power between two levels of government. Besides the federal government in Ottawa, each of the ten Canadian provinces, including Ontario, elect their own governments with the power to legislate in certain areas. Based on the British model, the political systems in Canada and Ontario give legislative power to parliaments elected by universal suffrage. The political party with the greatest number of elected members forms the government except in very rare cases when very close results enable the government to be formed by a coalition between the second-place and third-place parties. This is what happened after the 1985 Ontario election when the Liberal Party obtained the support of the New Democratic Party to prevent the Conservatives from forming the government even though the Conservatives had won more seats than either of the other two parties on their own.

Elections are usually held every four years, but a government can prolong its mandate for up to five years. Unlike the system in the United States, the party in power decides on the timing of elections, which are based on a simple majority in single-member constituencies. As in Britain, this usually leads to battles between only two strong parties.

On the federal scene, two political parties, the Liberal Party and the Progressive Conservative Party, have traditionally taken turns governing Canada ever since Confederation in 1867. The current Canadian prime minister, Jean Chrétien, was elected under the Liberal banner in 1993 and again in 1997. He succeeded Conservative Prime Minister Brian Mulroney, who had won the 1984 and 1988 federal elections before giving up his post to the party's new leader Kim Campbell near the end of his second mandate.

In Canadian political history, the 1993 federal election was doubtless a watershed, for it led to an unprecedented realignment of the political spectrum, with the Conservatives and New Democrats nearly wiped out and the representation of two new parties, the Bloc Québécois and the Reform Party, the former assuming the role of the opposition. The 1997 federal elections brought all five parties to the fore, with the liberals again winning most of the seats.

As for provincial politics, the Conservative party has traditionally held sway in Ontario. In fact, between 1943 and 1985, the province was governed without interruption by Conservative premiers. Although they have had to make compromises, especially at times of minority governments, the Conservatives have never been very warm to the idea of promoting the interests of women, the poor or minorities such as the numerous French-speaking people in the northern part of the province. The 1985 election put an end to the long Conservative reign in Ontario, though the results still favoured the Conservatives, who won 52 seats against 48 for the Liberals and 25 for the New Democrats. It took a coalition between David Peterson's Liberals and Bob Rae's New Democrats to end nearly a half-century of Conservative rule in Ontario.

Peterson became premier of the province and enacted a proactive law on equal wages for women. Two important matters greatly reduced his popularity with the electorate, however. One was the Free Trade Agreement with the United States. The other was the Meech Lake Accord, which sought to offer Québec a special status within the Canadian Confederation but which two provinces failed to ratify. Peterson was opposed to the Free Trade Agreement but could not persuade the federal government to back off on this deal that a majority of Ontarians saw as negative for their province's economic development. As for Meech Lake, which eventually fell through, Peterson gave it his support despite opposition from many people in Ontario.

PORTRAIT

Peterson was beaten in the 1990 provincial election but, to almost everyone's surprise, he was replaced by the New Democrats, lead by a brilliant intellectual, Bob Rae. During their years in coalition with the Liberals, Rae and his party had succeeded in ridding the party of its left-wing image, thereby winning the confidence of many Ontarians. Rae's five years as premier turned out to be very difficult, however, because of a harsh economic recession which lead to an increase in the province's debt. Like his predecessor, Rae was to hold power for only five years. In 1995, he was replaced by Mike Harris of the Conservative party, the essence of whose platform was to fight tooth and nail against the deficit through radical cuts in government services.

ECONOMY

The economy of the Ottawa region is largely dependent on the federal civil service, which, both directly and indirectly, employs a large percentage of the local workforce. Generally speaking, the civil service provides stability in the employment sector and also allows for a particularly large middle class. The annual household income, furthermore, is above the national average. This traditional stability has been threatened somewhat in recent years by government cutbacks aiming to reduce the federal deficit. The service sector also provides jobs, particularly in the computer and insurance industries. The Rideau Valley is still the area best-suited to farming in the Ottawa region, and the forest industry still plays a major role in the economy, especially on the Québec side.

ARTS

In 50 years, Bytown grew from a small community of a few thousand people to a sizable city, leading to a major growth in its population. This metamorphosis brought about extensive changes in the town, which saw the construction of handsome government buildings and then the improvement of its public services. All this activity also had an impact on the local arts scene, which was gradually taking shape.

The mid-19th century saw the flowering of the arts scene in both the Francophone and Anglophone communities, whose cultural institutions developed at the same time. In the Anglophone community, this flowering manifested itself primarily in the creation of various organizations, such as The Mechanics Institute and Athenaeum (1853), The Natural History Society of Ottawa (1863) and The Ottawa Field Naturalists Club, which later became The Arts and Letters Club. All three contributed to the community's cultural vitality.

The Institut Canadien Français d'Ottawa, run by a religious order in those days, was the centre of musical, theatrical and literary activity in the Francophone community. This institute later became the Collège d'Ottawa and the Université d'Ottawa. This group of French-speaking intellectuals, led by local religious communities, soon focussed on defending the rights of Francophones. The creation of a French-language education system, directed by Catholic communities, was among their demands. This subject caused a great deal of controversy, since it put the Anglophone Catholic community in a quandary. A serious social debate ensued. In order to defend their views, the Francophones founded a newspaper, *Le Droit*, in 1913. In 1918, the two communities reached a compromise; the administration of primary schools would be divided between English- and French-speaking Catholics. It wasn't until 1968, however, that the Ontario government agreed to create public high schools for French-language education. Prior to that, the religious communities had established private schools, so only a privileged few had access to education in french.

Though the city's communities were constantly in conflict, right from the start there was a common desire to equip Ottawa with cultural institutions worthy of a national capital. In 1894, the city's first symphony orchestra, composed mainly of amateur musicians, was founded, but like many of the other little groups that emerged on the arts scene around that time, it succumbed to financial difficulties eight years later. It was succeeded by other orchestras, but they all met similar fates. It wasn't until many years later that any real effort was made to develop the city's cultural scene. Finally, in 1965-1966, the Ottawa Symphony Orchestra was founded. The fact that it was so difficult, if not impossible, to find a venue in which to perform prevented many smaller orchestras and theatre companies from flourishing. Only the Ottawa Little Theatre, founded in 1912, managed to find a home and survive; they are still performing popular plays to this day. The construction of the National Arts Centre in 1969 was a milestone. Devoted to the performing arts, this centre has three theatres, where top-quality plays, dance performances and concerts given by the house orchestra are presented. The capital area also boasts several prestigious museums, including the Canadian Museum of Civilization, in Hull, and the National Gallery of Canada, which have been instrumental in drawing attention to Canadian artists and culture.

ARCHITECTURE

When Ottawa was founded in 1827, it had only been about 50 years since British colonists fleeing the newly independent United States settled west of the Ottawa River, in Ontario. These new arrivals, confronting a vast, almost virgin territory, preserved their architectural traditions; Georgian houses made of hewn stone, built according to a very specific, symmetrical design, gradually appeared on the horizon. These lovely houses still grace the Ottawa Valley. Though few remain in Ottawa, some examples can still be found, one being Louis Besserer's house (see p 86). Buildings dating back to the city's beginnings are rare. Aside from a few impressive projects like the Rideau Canal, little back then was built to last.

Rigorous adhesion to the Georgian style was gradually abandoned in favour of various styles inspired by trends of the past. Though very different from one another, these styles all emerged during the reign of Queen Victoria (1837-1901) and thus are all lumped together under the heading of "Victorian architecture". This was an important period in the history of Ottawa, which was named the capital of United Canada in 1857, then of Canada in 1867; with this change of status, the city began to undergo a transformation.

Though a few handsome neo-Gothic buildings had already been erected along the Ottawa River (Earnscliffe, see p 87), the construction of the Parliament Buildings set off a rage for this style, characterized by gothic arches, pinnacles and crenellations. During the second half of the 19th century, the

Earnscliffe

neo-Gothic style was used for many government buildings and churches; indeed, to some extent, it shaped the face of the capital.

Though neo-Gothic was the most popular style of the second half of the 19th century, other styles, notably Queen Anne, distinguished by gables, dormer windows and asymmetrical lines, emerged in residential architecture. The Second Empire style, associated with Parisian sophistication under Napoleon III and characterized by the use of mansard roofs, among other features, was also used for a number of public buildings (Langevin Block, see p 71).

In the 20th century, Victorian architecture remained in fashion but was toned down. Then, little by little, another style emerged to change the face of the capital once again, the

Château style, inspired by French châteaux of the 14th and 15th centuries, particularly those of the Loire Valley. The first building in Ottawa designed in this style was the Château Laurier, erected on the banks of the Ottawa River in 1912. This aesthetic quickly gained favour with the federal government, which believed that it reflected just the right image for the nation's capital. A number of government buildings went up in the first few years of the 20th century. In order to make them blend in harmoniously with existing buildings, they were designed in an original combination of the Chateau and neo-Gothic styles, lending the city a distinctive appearance (Confederation Building, see p 72).

As Ottawa entered the modern era, newer architectural trends gradually emerged. Among these was the Art-Deco style, used, most prominently, for banks and other financial institutions. Adaptations of that style can also be found; the Supreme Court of Canada, for example, features a blend of the Art Deco and Chateau styles.

The 1960s marked another turning point for the city. Not only were the roads redesigned to improve the flow of traffic around the Rideau Canal, but thanks to a new law, it was now permissible to erect buildings taller than those of Parliament. Bit by bit, concrete, glass and steel skyscrapers appeared on the skyline – not always embellishing it. In the 1980s, the beautification of the nation's capital became a central concern, and a program designed to achieve that end – by creating new parks and erecting magnificent buildings like the National Gallery of Canada and the Canadian Museum of Civilization – was launched.

A FEW FAMOUS OTTAWANS

After serving in the British army against France and Spain, **George Ramzay Dalhousie** (1770-1838) came to Canada to serve in Nova Scotia. His main claim to fame was as governor of British North America from 1820 to 1828. We have Dalhousie to thank for the Rideau Canal, since it was he who, in 1823, purchased 160 hectares of land west of the Rideau River and south of the Ottawa River so that the canal could be dug. In some way, he is the father of Ottawa.

Lieutenant-Colonel **John By** (1779-1836) entered military academy in 1797. In 1802, he was sent to Canada, where he helped build the locks on the St. Lawrence River and the fortifications of Québec City. In 1811, he returned to England to fight Spain and France. In 1826, this brilliant, seasoned engineer, who was 47 at the time, was called back to Canada and placed in charge of the construction of the Rideau Canal. In addition to supervising this project, he furthered the development of the little village taking shape there, which was named Bytown in his honour. Despite these efforts, his career ended on a regrettable note: when the canal ended up going way over budget, he was called back to England to answer accusations that he had mismanaged the funds.

A poor Irish immigrant, **Nicholas Sparks** first settled in Wrightown (now Hull), where he worked as a farmer. In 1821, he bought 80 hectares of relatively worthless land covered with trees and stones on the south bank of the Ottawa River for the sum of 95 pounds. When he made this purchase, he had no idea that the land would increase in value. A few years later, the Rideau Canal was dug right alongside his vast piece of property. As Bytown developed, Sparks got rich leasing out plots of land. He is also known for his many efforts to encourage economic growth in Upper Town, which had developed on his land.

Only one other person owned land alongside the Rideau Canal, his on the east side. **Louis Besserer** did not play as prominent a role as Sparks, since he did not subdivide his land until the second half of the 19th century, when Ottawa, by then the nation's capital, was booming.

John A. Macdonald (1815-1891) was elected to the Legislative Assembly of United Canada for the first time in 1844, then re-elected in 1848, 1851, 1854, 1857, 1861 and 1863. Starting in 1864, he played a vital role in the creation of the Canadian Confederation. In 1867, he was elected the first federal prime minister. Except for 1875, when his government had to step down in the wake of a scandal, he held that office until his death in 1891.

Wilfrid Laurier (1841-1919), a Liberal, was first elected to federal office in 1874. He was appointed minister in 1878 and became leader of the opposition in 1887. A great speaker and negotiator, he became the first French Canadian to be elected prime minister of Canada. Even in his first years in office, he had great plans for Ottawa, which he wanted to make the "Washington of the North". During his terms as prime minister, considerable efforts were made to beautify the capital, with no fewer than 11 stately buildings going up, among them the Château Laurier, the Royal Canadian Mint and the Connaught Building. He lived in Ottawa right up until his death, and his house is open to the public (see p 87).

William Lyon Mackenzie King (1874-1950) succeeded Wilfrid Laurier as leader of the Liberal Party in 1919. A Doctor of Political Science, he spent part of his career in the civil service, specializing in labour-related issues. Prime minister of Canada from 1921 to 1930 and from 1935 to 1948, he, like Laurier, was keen on beautifying the nation's capital. To that end, he persuaded the Public Works Department to use the Château style for government buildings. His summer home in Kingsmere is open to the public (see p 102).

Architect **Thomas Fuller** (1823-1898), a native of England, started his career in Canada, in Toronto, where he joined forces with Chilion Jones. Both men soon earned themselves a solid reputation, particularly in the domain of church construction. In 1859, their design was selected for the main building on Parliament Hill in Ottawa. In 1881, Fuller was named head architect of the Department of Public Works. He was responsible for erecting some 140 buildings across the country and could thus be said to have shaped the face of Canada in his day.

David Ewart (1843-1921) was the head architect at the Department of Public Works from 1897 to 1914. He was in charge of erecting numerous government buildings all over the country, and several others in the capital, most notably the Royal Canadian Mint and the building that now houses the Canadian War Museum.

In 1882, **Archibald Lampman** (1861-1899) received a diploma in classics and joined the civil service as a clerk for the post office departement in Ottawa. A great observer of nature who developed a personal style influenced by the Romantic Movement, he was one of the greatest Canadian poets of the late 19th century. He died young, having published only two collections of poems, *Among the Millet* (1888) and *Lyrics of Earth* (1895); a third, *Alcyone and Other Poems* was about to come out when he passed away.

Duncan Campbell Scott (1862-1947), a friend of Archibald Lampman's, also worked in the civil service in Ottawa, for the Ministry of Indian Affairs. Upon Lampman's advice, Scott also devoted himself to writing. In the course of his lengthy career, he published short stories, novels and essays but remains best known as a poet.

Margaret Atwood (1939-) spent her early childhood in Ottawa. Her family moved to Toronto when she was seven, and she has since lived in a number of North American cities, including Boston, Montréal and Vancouver. A talented poet, critic, novelist and short story writer, she has created a very personal body of work. In 1965, she won Canada's most important literary prize, the Governor General's Award, for *The Circle Game*, a collection of poems. A prolific author, she has since published about 20 other works, many of which have enjoyed great success. Her work is marked by a critical, sometimes satirical view of society and an activist stance in regard to feminism and various other causes. Atwood has also earned a name for herself as a television writer, having been involved in a number of series.

The popular singer and songwriter **Paul Anka** (1941-) has recorded a number of hit songs himself, such as *You Are My Destiny*, and composed many others for such renowned fellow artists as Frank Sinatra (*My Way*). With more than 400 songs to his name, he was one of the most famous Canadian singers and songwriters in the world in his heyday.

Bruce Cockburn (1945-) was born in Ottawa and spent a good part of his childhood on a farm in the area. This experience stayed with him, and his feelings about rural life are reflected in the lyrics of his early albums. Influenced as a child by rock legends like Elvis Presley, Bob Dylan and John Lennon, Cockburn later studied harmony and composition at the Berkeley School of Music in Boston, then spent some time performing on the streets of Paris before returning to his home town. In the late 1960s, he adopted a much more acoustic sound, which he never abandoned. To date, this pop star has recorded about 20 albums and has received countless awards for his music.

Born in Ottawa to a French Canadian father and a Hungarian mother, **Alanis Nadine Morissette** (1974-) is one of the most successful Canadian singers of the 1990s. Her first album, recorded when she was just 17, won the Juno Award for most promising female singer. Though already off to a good start before, she attained true celebrity status in 1995, at the age of 21, with her album *Jagged Little Pill*, which won all sorts of awards, including the coveted Grammy for album of the year.

Dan Aykroyd (1952-) was born in Ottawa, where his parents, Peter Samuel Gilbert and Lorraine Gougeon, were federal civil servants. He spent his entire youth in Ottawa and even enrolled in university here. He began his career as a comedian in Canada before becoming a star as a member of the cast of the American television show *Saturday Night Live*. He later appeared in a number of popular American movies, including *The Blues Brothers* (1980), *Ghostbusters* (1984) and *Spies Like Us* (1985). Despite his success in the U.S., he has continued to work on television projects for the Canadian Broadcasting Corporation.

PRACTICAL INFORMATION

nformation in this chapter will help you to better plan your trip, not only well in advance, but once you've arrived in Ottawa. Important details on entrance formalities and other procedures, as well as general information, have been compiled for visitors from other countries and Canadians.

Ottawa's **area code** is **613**.

ENTRANCE FORMALITIES

Passports

A valid passport is usually sufficient for most visitors planning to stay less than three months; visas are not required. A three-month extension is possible, but a return ticket and proof of sufficient funds to cover this extension may be required.

Caution: some countries do not have an agreement with Canada concerning health and accident insurance, so it is advisable to have the appropriate coverage. For more information, see the section entitled **"Health"** on page 54.

Extended Visits

Visitors must submit a request to extend their visit **in writing** and **before** the expiration of their visa (the date is usually written in your passport) to an Immigration Canada office. To make a request you must have a valid passport, a return ticket, proof of sufficient funds to cover the stay, as well as the $65 non-refundable filing-fee. In some cases (work, study), however, the request must be made **before** arriving in Canada.

CUSTOMS

If you are bringing gifts into Canada, remember that certain restrictions apply. Smokers (minimum age is 16) can bring in a maximum of 200 cigarettes, 50 cigars, 400 grams of tobacco, or 400 tobacco sticks. For wine and alcohol the limit is 1.1 litres; in practice, however, two bottles per person are usually allowed. The limit for beer is twenty-four 355-ml size cans or bottles.

Plants, vegetation, and food: there are very strict rules regarding the importation of plants, flowers, and other vegetation; it is therefore not advisable to bring any of these types of products into the country. If it is absolutely necessary, contact the Customs-Agriculture service of the Canadian embassy **before** leaving your country.

Pets: if you are travelling with your pet, you will need a health certificate (available from your veterinarian) as well as a rabies vaccination certificate. It is important to remember that the vaccination must have been administered **at least 30 days before** your departure and should not be more than a year old.

Tax reimbursements for visitors: it is possible to be reimbursed for certain taxes paid on purchases made in Canada (see p 51).

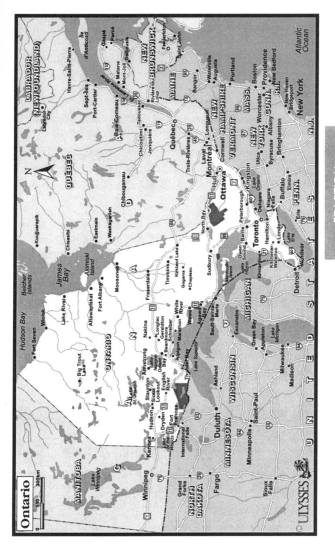

EMBASSIES AND CONSULATES

Canadian Embassies and Consulates Abroad

Australia
Canadian Consulate General: Level 5, Quay West, 111 Harrington Road, Sydney, N.S.W., Australia 2000, ☎(2) 9364-3000, ✆(2) 9364-3050.

Belgium
Canadian Embassy: 2 Avenue de Tervuren, 1040 Brussels, ☎(2) 741.06.11, ✆(2) 741.06.43, Métro Mérode.

Denmark
Canadian Embassy: Kr. Bernikowsgade 1, DK=1105 Copenhagen K, Denmark, ☎(45) 33.12.22.99, ✆(45) 33.14.05.85.

Finland
Canadian Embassy: Pohjos Esplanadi 25 B, 00100 Helsinki, Finland, ☎(9) 171-141, ✆(9) 601-060.

Germany
Canadian Consulate General: Internationales Handelzentrum, Friedrichstrasse 95, 23rd Floor, 10117 Berlin, Germany, ☎(30) 261.11.61, ✆(30) 262.92.06.

Great Britain
Canada High Commission: Macdonald House, One Grosvenor Square, London W1X 0AB, England, ☎(171) 258-6600, ✆(171) 258-6333.

Italy
Canadian Embassy: Via G.B. de Rossi 27, 00161 Rome, ☎(6) 44.59.81, ✆(6) 44.59.87.50.

Netherlands
Canadian Embassy: Sophialaan 7, 2514JP The Hague, Netherlands, ☎(70) 311-1600, ✆(70) 311-1682.

Norway
Canadian Embassy: Wergelandsveien 7, Oslo 0244, Norway, ☎(47) 22.99.53.00, ✉(47) 22.99.53.01.

Spain
Canadian Embassy: Edificio Goya, Calle Nuñez de Balboa 35, 28001 Madrid, ☎(1) 431.43.00, ✉(1) 435.74.88.

Sweden
Canadian Embassy: Tegelbacken 4, 7th floor, Box 16129, 10323 Stockholm, Sweden, ☎(8) 613-9900, ✉(8) 24.24.91.

Switzerland
Canadian Embassy: Kirchenfeldstrasse 88, 3000 Berne 6, ☎(31) 357.32.00, (31) ✉357.32.10.

United States
Canadian Embassy: 501 Pennsylvania Avenue, N.W., Washington, DC, 20001, ☎(202) 682-1740, ✉(202) 682-7726.

Canadian Consulate General: 1175 Peachtree Street NE, 100 Colony Square Suite 1700, Atlanta, Georgia, 30303-2705, ☎(404) 532-2000, ✉(404) 532-2050.

Canadian Consulate General: Three Copley Place, Suite 400, Boston, Massachusetts, 02116, ☎(617) 262-3760, ✉(617) 262-3415.

Canadian Consulate General: Two Prudential Plaza, 180 N. Stetson Avenue, Suite 2400, Chicago, Illinois, 60601, ☎(312) 616-1860, ✉(312) 616-1877.

Canadian Consulate General: St. Paul Place, 750 N. St. Paul Street, Suite 1700, Dallas, Texas, 75201, ☎(214) 922-9806, ✉(214) 922-9815.

Canadian Consulate General: 600 Renaissance Center, Suite 1100, Detroit, Michigan, 48234-1798, ☎(313) 567-2085, ✉(313) 567-2164.

Canadian Consulate General: 300 South Hope Street, 9th Floor, Los Angeles, California, 90071, ☎(213) 346-2700, ✉(213) 620-8827.

Canadian Consulate General: Suite 900, 701 Fourth Avenue South, Minneapolis, Minnesota, 55415-1899, ☎(612) 333-4641, ⊷(612) 332-4061.

Canadian Consulate General: 1251 Avenue of the Americas, New York, New York, 10020-1175, ☎(212) 596-1683, ⊷(212) 596-1790.

Canadian Consulate General: One Marine Midland Center, Suite 3000, Buffalo, New York, 14203-2884, ☎(716) 858-9500, ⊷(716) 852-4340.

Canadian Consulate General: 412 Plaza 600, Sixth and Stewart Streets, Seattle, Washington, 98101-1286, ☎(206) 443-1777, ⊷(206) 443-9662.

Foreign Embassies in Ottawa

Australia
Australian High Commission: 50 O'connor Street, Ottawa, Ontario, K1N 5R2, ☎236-0841, ⊷236-4376.

Belgium
Embassy: 80 Elgin Street, 4th Floor, Ottawa, Ontario, K1P 1B7, ☎236-7267, ⊷236-7882.

Denmark
Embassy: 47 Clarence, Ottawa, Ont., K1N 9K1, ☎562-1811

Finland
Embassy: 55 Metcalfe, Suite 850, Ottawa, Ont., K1P 6L5, ☎236-2389

Germany
Embassy: 1 Waverley, Ottawa, Ont., K2P 0T8, ☎232-1101, ⊷594-9330.

Great Britain
Embassy: 80 Elgin, Ottawa, Ont., K1P 5K7, ☎237-1303, ⊷237-6537.

Italy
Embassy: 275 Slater Street, 21st Floor, Ottawa, Ont., K1P 5H9, ☎232-2401, ≈233-1484.

Netherlands
Embassy: 350 Albert Street, Suite 2020, Ottawa, Ont., K1R 1A4, ☎237-5030, ≈237-6471.

Norway
Embassy: 90 Sparks, Ottawa, Ont., K1P 5B4, ☎238-6571.

Spain
Embassy: 74 Stanley Avenue, K1M 1P4, ☎747-2252, ≈744-1224.

Sweden
Embassy: 377 Dalhousie, Ottawa, Ont., K1N 9N8, ☎241-8553, ≈241-2277.

Switzerland
Embassy: 5 Malborough Avenue, K1N 8E6, ☎235-1837, ≈563-1394.

United States
Embassy: 100 Wellington, Ottawa, Ont., K1P 5T1, ☎238-5335, ≈238-5720.

PRACTICAL INFORMATION

TOURIST INFORMATION

A brand new tourist information office has just opened its doors a stone's throw from Parliament Hill. Brochures, information, hotel-room reservation centre... all the services you could possibly need are available here.

Capital Call Centre
90 Wellington Street, ☎239-5000 or (800) 465-1867.
End of May to early Sep, everyday, 8:30am to 9pm; rest of the year, everyday, 9am to 5pm.

You can also obtain a great deal of additional tourist-related information by checking out various websites. Here are a few:

www.capcan.ca
www.ottawakiosk.com
www.tourottawa.org

Tourist Offices Abroad

Belgium
Comission Canadienne du Tourisme: Rue Américaine 27, 1060 Bruxelles, ☎(2) 538-5792, ≈(2) 539-2433.

Germany
Canada Tourismusprogramm: Postfach 200 247, 63469 Maintal 2, Deutschland, ☎(49) 6181 45178, ≈6181 497558, www.dfait-maeci.gc.ca/~bonn/Tourism/eto2main.htm.

Great Britain
Visit Canada Centre: 62-65 Trafalgar Square, London, WC2N 5DT, ☎891 715000 (calls charged at 50p/minute), ≈(44) 171 389 1149,

Italy
Canadian Tourism Commission: Via Vittor Pisani 19, 20124 Milan, Italy, ≈(2) 6758-3900

Netherlands
Canadian Tourism Commission: Sophialaan 7, 2514 JP, The Hague, Netherlands, ≈(70) 3111682.

Norway
Geelmuyden. Kiese: Lilleakervn.2d, Postboks 362, N-1324 Lysaker, NORDICS, ≈(47) 22 13 03 04.

Switzerland
Welcome to Canada!: 22, Freihofstrasse, 8700 Küsnacht, ☎(1) 910 90 01, ≈910 38 24.

United States
Tour & Travel: 84-03 Chapin Pkwy, Floor 3, Jamaica Queens, New York 11432, ☎(718) 657-1727, ≈(718) 206-9114.

MC & IT: 420 East 55th Street, New York, NY 10022, ☎(212) 317-1711, ≈(212) 317-1881.

GUIDED TOURS

Those who are short of time but wish to get a good glimpse of the city's most attractive neighbourhoods can opt for a guided tour of Ottawa. A few companies offer worthwhile excursions through the streets of the capital.

Capital Double-Decker and Trolley Tours *($20)*
☎729-6888 or (800) 823-6147, ☏729-7444.
Departures: next to the Capital Call Centre

Gray Line *($16)*
☎725-1441 or (800) 440-0317.

 GETTING TO OTTAWA

By Plane

Flights from major Canadian cities to Ottawa are frequent and reliable, but often expensive. Travellers leaving from Montreal might consider taking the train or the bus, which is sometimes faster (about 2 hours' journey). From Europe, direct flights to Ottawa are rare, a number of them stop first in either Montreal or Toronto.

Macdonald-Cartier Airport

Ottawa's international airport *(50 Airport Dr.,* ☎*998-5213,* ☏*954-2136)* is small, but welcomes several fights a day from other Canadian cities and different countries. It is located about twenty minutes from downtown and easily reached by car (there are a number of car-rental companies here), by taxi or by bus (OC Transpo 96).

By car, you can reach downtown Ottawa via Airport Drive.

Airlines

Air Canada: ☎247-5000

American Airlines: 624 Bank Street, ☎(800) 624-5620, ⊷567-5609

Canadian Airlines: ☎237-1380

In Ontario

The **NorOntario** airline offers flights within the province to cities such as Sudbury, Sault-Sainte-Marie, Thunder Bay and Timmins. It is a subsidiary of Air Canada; for more information, you can call one of the airline's offices or dial ☎(705) 472-4500, ext. 358.

By Bus

Extensive and inexpensive, buses cover most of Canada. Except for public transportation, there is no government run service; several companies service the country. Gray Coach, Greyhound and Voyageur Colonial all serve the Ontario region.

Moreover, bus service, from Montreal and Toronto, is both rapid and punctual, and departures are frequent.

Ottawa Bus Station:

265 Catherine Street, ☎238-5900.

From the bus station, you can get to the downtown area by bus (OC Transpo 4) or by car via Kent or Bank Streets.

Smoking is forbidden on almost all lines and pets are not allowed. Generally children five years old or younger travel for free and people aged 60 or over are eligible for discounts.

The RoutPass

The various bus companies offer what is called a RoutPass; it is a single ticket that allows unlimited travel throughout most of Ontario and all of Québec. The ticket costs $199 and is valid for 14 days from May 1 to October 29. The ticket can be extended for up to six days for $19.37 a day. The extension must be purchased at the same time as the RoutPass, however. The RoutPass is less expensive if it is purchased in the pre-sale period from March 1 to April 22. Children under 12 get a 50% reduction, and children under 5 travel for free. The RoutPass is available at the above-mentioned stations.

By Train

VIA Rail transports passengers between the various Canadian provinces and serves several cities in southern and northern Ontario. This is without a doubt the most pleasant way of travelling from Montreal or Toronto to the capital. You will thus be treated to a comfortable ride while being waited on hand and foot.

The Ottawa train station is located a dozen minutes by car from the downtown area and is served by a good road network and public transport.

Ottawa Train Station
200 Tremblay Road, ☎244-1660

To get there by car, take the eastbound 417. The station is located a short distance past Riverside Drive.

Those opting for public transportation can take the OC Transpo's bus no. 95, which runs from the station to downtown, stopping right near Parliament Hill. A ticket costs $1,85.

You can also take a taxi from the station. The ride downtown should cost you under $10.

The Routes

Modern and rapid (reaching up to 150 km/h), VIA Rail trains connect eastern Canadian cities in no time.

Preferred by businesspeople, the Québec-Windsor corridor, one of the busiest routes, connects downtown of Québec, Montréal, Ottawa, Toronto, Windsor and other towns quickly and comfortably.

Economy or First Class?

Economy class carriages are equipped with comfortable seats and wide aisles and, for a slight surcharge, passengers can have something to eat as well. If you enjoy being waited on hand and foot, opt for first class, where the price of your ticket includes access to a waiting room, priority boarding and meals served with wine and spirits at your seat, in warmly decorated carriages.

Some trains are equipped with a Skyline carriage in which a café and saloon car allow you to enjoy yourselves in the company of other passengers. These carriages have large panoramic windows whence you can admire the passing landscape.

VIA offers several types of savings:

Up to 40% off on travel outside peak periods and tourist season, on certain days of the week and on advance bookings (five days), depending on the destination;

Student rebates (24 years and under, 40% year-round on advance booking except during Christmas period);

A 10% discount for people aged 60 and over, on certain days during off-peak travel times up to 50%, depending on the destination;

Special rates for children (2 to 11 years, half-price; free for 2 years and under, accompanied by an adult).

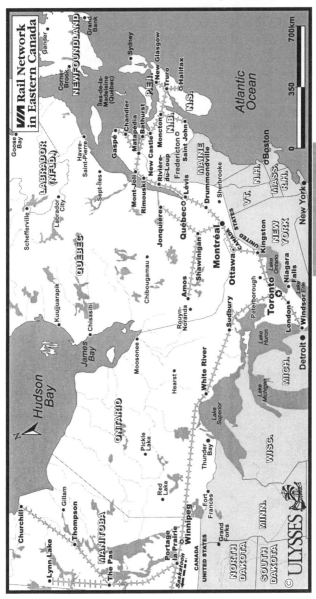

Special Tickets

With the **CANRAILPASS**, you can travel throughout Canada on one ticket. The ticket allows 12 days of unlimited travel in a 30-day period for $569 in high season and $369 in low season (Jan 1 to May 31 and Oct 16 to Dec 31).

The **North America Rail Pass**, valid on all *VIA* and *Amtrak* trains, is available in economy class for a 30-day period for $625 during off-peak periods and $895 during peak periods.

For further information, call your travel agent or closest *VIA* office, or visit the website at: www.viarail.ca

In Switzerland: Western Tours,
☎(01) 268 2323, ⚟(01) 268 2373.

In Canada: ☎1-800-561-8630 or contact your travel agent.

In Australia: Asia Pacific/Walshes World,
☎(02) 9318 1044, ⚟(02) 9318 2753.

In Italy: Gastaldi Tours, ☎(10) 24 511, ⚟(10) 28 0354.

In the Netherlands: Incento B.V.,
☎(035) 69 55111, ⚟(035) 69 55155.

In New Zealand: Walshes World,
☎(09) 379-3708, ⚟(09) 309-0725.

In the United Kingdom: Leisurail,
☎01733-335-599, ⚟01733-505-451.

In the United States: ☎(800) 561-3949 or contact your travel agent.

FINDING YOUR WAY AROUND

By Car

An excellent system of highways and expressways makes Ottawa easy to reach from many points in Ontario and Quebec.

From Toronto, follow Highway 7, which crosses Peterborough and goes directly to Ottawa. It is also possible to drive along the St. Lawrence, taking Highway 401 to Prescott and, from there, Highway 16 to Ottawa.

From Montréal, take Highway 40 and then the 417, and get off at the Nicholas St. exit to reach the downtown area.

PRACTICAL INFORMATION

Things to Consider

Driver's License: As a general rule, foreign driver's licenses are valid for six months from the arrival date in Canada.

Winter Driving: Although roads are generally in good condition, the dangers brought on by drastic climatic conditions must be taken into consideration. Roads are often transformed into virtual skating rinks by black ice. Wind is also a factor, causing blowing snow, and reducing visibility to almost nil. All these factors, which Canada is used to, require prudent driving. If you plan on driving through remote areas, be sure to bring along a blanket and some supplies should your car break down.

Driving and the Highway Code: There is no priority to the right. Traffic lights at intersections indicate priority to the right. Signs marked "Arrêt" or "Stop" against a red background must always be respected. Come to a complete stop even if there is no apparent danger.

Traffic lights are often located on the opposite side of the intersection, so be careful to stop on the stop line, a white line on the pavement before the intersection. When a school bus (usually yellow in colour) has stopped and has its signals flashing, you must come to a complete stop, no matter what

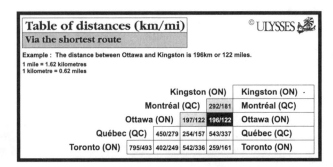

Table of distances (km/mi)
Via the shortest route

Example : The distance between Ottawa and Kingston is 196km or 122 miles.
1 mile = 1.62 kilometres
1 kilometre = 0.62 miles

				Kingston (ON) ·
		Kingston (ON)		
		Montréal (QC)	292/181	Montréal (QC)
	Ottawa (ON)	197/122	196/122	Ottawa (ON)
Québec (QC)	450/279	254/157	543/337	Québec (QC)
Toronto (ON) 795/493	402/249	542/336	259/161	Toronto (ON)

direction you are travelling in. Failing to stop at the flashing signals is considered a serious offense, and carries a heavy penalty. Wearing of seatbelts in the front and back seats is compulsory at all times.

In all provinces except for Québec, right turns are permitted on red lights as long as there are no cars in the right lane.

The speed limit on highways is 100 km/h. The speed limit on secondary highways is 90 km/h, and 50 km/h in urban areas.

Gas Stations: Because Canada produces its own crude oil, gasoline prices are less expensive than in Europe, around $0.60 a litre. Some gas stations (especially in the downtown areas) might ask for payment in advance as a security measure, especially after 11 p.m.

Accidents and Emergencies

In case of serious accident, fire or other emergency, you can dial **911**.

If you run into trouble on the highway, pull onto the shoulder of the road and turn the hazard lights on. If it is a rental car, contact the rental company as soon as possible. Always file an accident report. If a disagreement arises over who was at fault in an accident, ask for police help.

Car Rentals

Many travel agencies have agreements with the major car rental companies (Avis, Budget, Hertz, etc.) and offer good values; contracts often include added bonuses (reduced ticket prices for shows, etc.).

When renting a car, find out if:

The contract includes unlimited kilometres and if the insurance offered provides full coverage (accident, property damage, hospital costs for you and passengers, theft).

Car rental companies:

Avis
449 Gladstone St.
☎230-2847

Discount
161 Laurier Ave. W.
☎234-0814

Budget
☎729-6666

Hertz
881 St. Laurent Blvd
☎746-6683

PRACTICAL INFORMATION

Caution:

To rent a car, you must be at least 21 years of age and have had a driver's license for **at least** one year. If you are between 21 and 25, certain companies (for example Avis, Thrifty, Budget) will ask for a $500 deposit, and in some cases they will also charge an extra sum for each day you rent the car. These conditions do not apply for those over 25 years of age.

A credit card is extremely useful for the deposit to avoid tying up large sums of money.

Most rental cars have an automatic transmission, however you can request a car with a manual shift. Child safety seats cost extra.

Hitchhiking

There are two types: "free" hitchhiking, which is prohibited on highways, and "organized" hitchhiking with a group called Allo-Stop. "Free" hitchhiking is more common, especially during the summer, and easier to do outside the large city centres, but it is not recommended

"Organized" hitchhiking, or ridesharing, with **Allo-Stop** *(☎562-8248)* works very well in all seasons. This efficient company pairs drivers who want to share their car for a small payment with passengers needing a ride. A membership card is required and costs $6 for a passenger and $7 for a driver per year. The driver receives part (approximately 60 %) of the fees paid by the passengers. Destinations include virtually everywhere in the province of Québec, as well as the rest of Canada and the United States.

Children under five cannot travel with Allo-Stop because of a regulation requiring the use of child safety-seats. Not all drivers accept smokers, and not all passengers want to be exposed to smoke, so check on this ahead of time.

Public Transportation

The city of Ottawa boasts an efficient public transport network. Indeed, there is bus service to any destination in the capital's downtown area. Information concerning the various bus lines is readily available by contacting:

OC Transpo: 1500 St. Laurent Blvd., ☎741-4390, www.octranspo.com

The price for a bus ticket for an adult, senior citizen, student or teenager (over 12 years old) is $1,85; the fare for children of 6 to 11 years of age is $1; children under 6 ride for free.

$ MONEY AND BANKING

Exchange

Most banks readily exchange American and European currencies but almost all will charge **commission**. There are, however, exchange offices that do not charge commissions and have longer hours. Just remember to **ask about fees** and **to compare rates**.

Traveller's Cheques

Traveller's cheques are accepted in most large stores and hotels, however it is easier and to your advantage to change your cheques at an exchange office. For a better exchange rate buy your traveller's cheques in Canadian dollars before leaving.

Credit Cards

Most major credit cards are accepted at stores, restaurants and hotels. While the main advantage of credit cards is that they allow visitors to avoid carrying large sums of money, using a credit card also makes leaving a deposit for car rental much easier and some cards, gold cards for example, automatically insure you when you rent a car (check with your credit card company to see what coverage it provides). In addition, the exchange rate with a credit card is generally better. The most commonly accepted credit cards are Visa, MasterCard, and American Express.

Banks

Banks can be found almost everywhere and most offer the standard services to tourists. Visitors who choose to stay for a long period of time should note that **non-residents** cannot open bank accounts. If this is the case, the best way to have money readily available is to use traveller's cheques. With-

Exchange Rates		
$1 US =	$1.43 CAN	$1 CAN = $0.69 US
1 £ =	$2.40 CAN	$1 CAN = £0.41
$1 Aust =	$0.93 CAN	$1 CAN = $1.07 Aust
$1 NZ =	$0.79 CAN	$1 CAN = $1.25 NZ
1 Euro =	$1.62 CAN	$1 CAN = $0.62 Euro
1 fl =	$0.71 CAN	$1 CAN = 1.40 fl
1 SF =	$0.96 CAN	$1 CAN = 1.04 SF
10 BF =	$0.40 CAN	$1 CAN = 25.76 BF
1 DM =	$0.80 CAN	$1 CAN = 1.24 DM
10 pesetas =	$0.10 CAN	$1 CAN = 105 pesetas
1000 lire =	$0.80 CAN	$1 CAN = 1233 lire

drawing money from foreign accounts is expensive. However, several automatic teller machines accept foreign bank cards, so that you can withdraw directly from your account. Money orders are another means of having money sent from abroad. No commission is charged but it takes time. People who have residence status, permanent or not (such as landed-immigrants, students), can open a bank account. A passport and proof of residence status are required.

CURRENCY

The monetary unit is the dollar ($), which is divided into cents (¢). One dollar = 100 cents.

Bills come in 2, 5, 10, 20, 50, 100, 500 and 1000 dollar denominations, and coins come in 1 (pennies), 5 (nickels), 10 (dimes) and 25 (quarters) cent pieces, and in 1 (loonies) dollar and 2 dollar coins.

TAXES AND TIPPING

Taxes

The ticket price on items usually **does not include tax**. In Ontario there are two taxes, the G.S.T or federal Goods and Services Tax, of 7%, which is payable in throughout Canada, and a provincial sales tax of 8%.

Tax Reimbursements for Non-Residents

Non-residents can be refunded for taxes paid on their purchases made while in Canada. To obtain a refund, it is important to keep your receipts. A separate form for each tax (federal and provincial) must be filled out to obtain a refund. Conditions under which refunds are awarded are different for the GST and the PST. For further information, call ☎1-800-668-4748 (for GST).

Tipping

Tipping applies to all table services, that is in restaurants or other places in which customers are served at their tables (fast food service is therefore not included in this category). Tipping is also compulsory in bars, nightclubs and taxis.

Depending on the quality of the service, patrons must give approximately 15% of the bill before tax. Unlike in Europe, the tip is not included in the bill, and clients must calculate the amount themselves and give it to the waitress or waiter; service and tip are one and the same in North America.

TIME DIFFERENCE

Almost all of Ontario is in the same time zone (Eastern Time). The part of the province to the west of Thunder Bay falls in another time zone (Central Time) which is one hour behind the

PRACTICAL INFORMATION

rest of the province. The majority of the province is therefore six hours behind continental Europe and five hours behind the United Kingdom. Daylight Savings Time (+ 1 hour) begins the first Sunday in April and ends the last Sunday in October. Furthermore, do not forget that there are several time zones in Canada, for example when in it noon in Ottawa, it is 9am in Vancouver.

BUSINESS HOURS AND PUBLIC HOLIDAYS

Business Hours

Stores

Generally stores remain open the following hours:

Mon to Fri	10am to 6pm;
Thu and Fri	10am to 9pm;
Sat	9 am or 10am to 5pm;
Sun	noon to 5pm

Well-stocked stores that sell food, sometimes called convenience stores or variety stores, are found throughout Ontario and are open later, sometimes 24 hours a day.

Banks

Banks are open Monday to Friday from 10am to 3pm. Most are open on Thursdays and Fridays, until 6pm or even 8pm. Automatic teller machines are widely available and are open night and day.

Post Offices

Large post offices are open Monday to Friday from 9am to 5pm. There are also several smaller post offices located in shopping malls, convenience stores, and even pharmacies; these post offices are open much later than the larger ones.

Holidays and Public Holidays

The following is a list of public holidays in the Ontario. Most administrative offices and banks are closed on these days.

New Year's Day and day after:	January 1 and 2
Good Friday or Easter Monday	
Victoria Day:	3rd Monday in May
Canada Day:	July 1st
Civic holiday:	1st Monday in August
Labour Day:	1st Monday in September
Thanksgiving:	2nd Monday in October
Remembrance Day:	November 1
	(only banks and federal government services are closed)
Christmas Day:	December 25

PRACTICAL INFORMATION

CLIMATE AND CLOTHING

Ontario has a continental climate, with very defined season. In summer the temperature can reach 30°C, while in the winter it can drop to -25°C and snow is common and often very abundant. In spring and fall, the sun is often hidden behind rain clouds.

Winter

December to March is the ideal season for winter-sports enthusiasts (skiing, skating, etc.). Warm clothing is essential during this season (coat, scarf, hat, gloves, wool sweaters and boots). Toronto and the southwestern part of the province generally benefit from slightly milder conditions than the rest of southern Ontario.

Spring and Fall

Spring is short (end of March to end of May) and is characterized by a general thaw leading to wet and muddy conditions. Fall is often cool. A sweater, scarf, gloves, windbreaker and umbrella will therefore come in handy.

Summer

Summer lasts from the end of May to the end of August and can be very hot. Bring along t-shirts, lightweight shirts and pants, shorts and sunglasses; a sweater or light jacket is a good idea for evenings.

HEALTH

Vaccinations are not necessary for people coming from Europe, the United States, Australia and New Zealand. On the other hand, it is strongly suggested, particularly for medium or long-term stays, that visitors take out health and accident insurance. There are different types so it is best to shop around. Bring along all medication, especially prescription medicine. Unless otherwise stated, the water is drinkable throughout Ontario.

In the winter, moisturizing lotion and lip balm are useful for people with sensitive skin, since the air in many buildings is very dry.

During the summer, always protect yourself against sunburn. It is often hard to feel your skin getting burned by the sun on windy days. Do not forget to bring sun screen!

Canadians from outside Ontario should take note that in general your province's health care system will only reimburse you for the cost of any hospital fees or procedures at the going rate in your province. For this reason, it is a good idea to get extra private insurance. In case of accident or illness make sure to keep your receipts in order to be reimbursed by your province's health care system.

EMERGENCIES

The ☎ **911** emergency number is in operation throughout most of Ontario. If it does not work dial **0** and tell the operator that this is an emergency.

INSURANCE

Cancellation Insurance

Your travel agent will usually offer you cancellation insurance upon purchase of your airline ticket or vacation package. This insurance allows you to be reimbursed for the ticket or package deal if your trip must be cancelled due to serious illness or death. Healthy people are unlikely to need this protection, which is therefore only of relative use.

Theft Insurance

Most residential insurance policies protect some of your goods from theft, even if the theft occurs in a foreign country. To make a claim, you must fill out a police report. It may not be necessary to take out further insurance, depending on the amount covered by your current home policy. As policies vary considerably, you are advised to check with your insurance company. European visitors should take out baggage insurance.

Life Insurance

Several airline companies offer a life insurance plan included in the price of the airplane ticket. However, many travellers already have this type of insurance and do not require additional coverage.

PRACTICAL
INFORMATION

Health Insurance

This is the most useful kind of insurance for travellers, and should be purchased before your departure. Your insurance plan should be as complete as possible because health care costs add up quickly. When buying insurance, make sure it covers all types of medical costs, such as hospitalization, nursing services and doctor's fees. Make sure your limit is high enough, as these expenses can be costly. A repatriation clause is also vital in case the required care is not available on site. Furthermore, since you may have to pay immediately, check your policy to see what provisions it includes for such situations. To avoid any problems during your vacation, always keep proof of your insurance policy on your person.

TELECOMMUNICATIONS

The **area code** of Ottawa and its surrounding region is **613**; for Hull it is **819**. Dialling this code is unnecessary if the call is local. For long distance calls, dial 1 for the United States and Canada, followed by the appropriate area code and the subscriber's number. Phone numbers preceded by 1-800 or 1-888 allow you to reach the subscriber without charge if calling from Canada, and often from the US as well. If you wish to contact an operator, dial **0**.

When calling abroad you can use a local operator and pay local phone rates. First dial 011 then the international country code and then the phone number.

Country codes :

United Kingdom:	44
Ireland:	353
Australia:	61
New Zealand:	64
Belgium:	32
Switzerland:	41
Italy:	39

Spain: 34
Netherlands: 31
Germany: 49

For example, to call Belgium, dial 011-32, followed by the area code (Antwerp 3, Brussels 2, Ghent 91, Liège 41) and the subscriber's number. To call Switzerland, dial 011-41, followed by the area code (Bern 31, Geneva 22, Lausanne 21, Zurich 1) and the subscriber's phone number.

Another way to call abroad is by using the direct access numbers below to contact an operator in your home country.

United States:
AT&T, ☎1-800-CALL ATT,
MCI, ☎1-800-888-8000
British Telecom Direct:
☎1-800-408-6420 or 1-800-363-4144
Australia Telstra Direct:
☎1-800-663-0683
New Zealand Telecom Direct: ☎1-800-663-0684

PRACTICAL
INFORMATION

Considerably less expensive to use than in Europe, public phones are scattered throughout the city, easy to use and some even accept credit cards. Local calls cost $0.25 for unlimited time. For long distance calls, equip yourselves with quarters ($0.25 coins), or purchase a $10, $15 or $20 phone card, on sale at newsstands. Calling a private residence will cost even less. Paying by credit card or with the prepaid "HELLO!" card is also possible, but be advised that calling by such means is considerably more expensive.

 SHOPPING

In most cases prices are fixed and as indicated. Do not be surprised, however, if you hear someone asking a store clerk if something is on sale.

What to Buy

Compact Discs: Compact discs are much less expensive than in Europe, however, they may be more expensive than in the United States.

Furs and Leather: Clothes made from animal skins are of very good quality and their prices are relatively low. Approximately 80% of fur items in Canada are made in the "fur area" of Montréal.

Local Arts & Crafts: These consist of paintings, sculptures, woodwork, ceramics, coppered enamel, weaving, etc.

Native Arts & Crafts: There are beautiful native sculptures made from different types of stone that are generally quite expensive. Make sure the sculpture is authentic by asking for a certificate of authenticity issued by the Canadian government. Good quality imitations are widely available and are much less expensive.

WINE, BEER AND ALCOHOL

The legal drinking age is 19. Beer, liquor and wine can only be purchased at the provincially run "Beer Store", "Liquor Store" and "Wine Store", respectively. These places are open quite late, until 10pm during the week and 11pm on Saturdays. Keep in mind that they are all closed on Sundays.

ADVICE FOR SMOKERS

As in the United States, cigarette smoking is considered taboo, and is being prohibited in more and more public places:

in most shopping centres;
in buses;
in government offices.

Most public places (restaurants, cafés) have smoking and non-smoking sections. Cigarettes are sold in bars, grocery stores, newspaper and magazine shops.

SAFETY

By taking the normal precautions, there is no need to worry about your personal security. If trouble should arise, remember to dial the emergency telephone number ☎ **911** or **0**.

CHILDREN

As in the rest of Canada, facilities exist in Ontario that make travelling with children quite easy, whether it be for getting around or when enjoying the sights. Generally children under five travel for free, and those under 12 are eligible for fare reductions. The same applies for various leisure activities and shows. Find out before you purchase tickets. High chairs and children's menus are available in most restaurants, while a few of the larger stores provide a babysitting service while parents shop.

HANDICAPPED TRAVELLERS

Though considerable efforts have been made to make things more accessible to handicapped individuals, there is still a lot of work to be done. To facilitate choosing your hotel, the &. symbol is included in the description of hotels that have special wheelchair access.

PETS

Ontario is generally quite tolerant of pets, which are permitted in all provincial parks as long as they are on a leash, and remember to properly dispose of their litter. Remember that animals are not allowed in grocery stores, restaurants or buses.

PRACTICAL
INFORMATION

WEIGHTS AND MEASURES

Although the metric system has been in use in Canada for several years, some people continue to use the Imperial system in casual conversation. Here a some equivalents:

Weights
1 pound (lb) = 454 grams (g)
1 kilogram (kg) = 2.2 pounds (lbs)

Linear Measure
1 inch = 2.54 centimetres (cm)
1 foot (ft) = 30 centimetres (cm)
1 mile = 1.6 kilometres (km)

Land Measure
1 acre = 0.4047 hectare
1 hectare = 2.471 acres

Volume Measure
1 U.S. gallon (gal) = 3.79 litres
1 U.S. gallon (gal) = 0.83 imperial gallon

Temperature
To convert °F into °C: subtract 32, divide by 9, multiply by 5
To convert °C into °F: multiply by 9, divide by 5, add 32.

GENERAL INFORMATION

Illegal Drugs: are against the law and not tolerated (even "soft" drugs). Anyone caught with drugs in their possession risks severe consequences.

Electricity: Voltage is 110 volts throughout Canada, the same as in the United States. Electricity plugs have two parallel, flat pins, and adaptors are available here.

Laundromats: are found almost everywhere in urban areas. In most cases, detergent is sold on site. Although change machines are sometimes provided, it is best to bring plenty of quarters (25¢) with you.

Movie Theatres: There are no ushers and therefore no tips.

Museums: Most museums charge admission. Reduced prices are available for people over 60, for children, and for students. Call the museum for further details.

Newspapers: *Ottawa Citizen; Le Droit* (French paper); *X Press* (free weekly cultural paper); *Xtra!* (Gay paper).

Pharmacies: In addition to the smaller drug stores, there are large pharmacy chains taht sell everything from chocolate to laundry detergent, as well as the more traditional items like cough drops and headache medications.

Religion: Almost all religions are represented.

Restrooms: Public restrooms can be found in most shopping centres. If you cannot find one, it usually is not a problem to use one in a bar or restaurant.

PRACTICAL INFORMATION

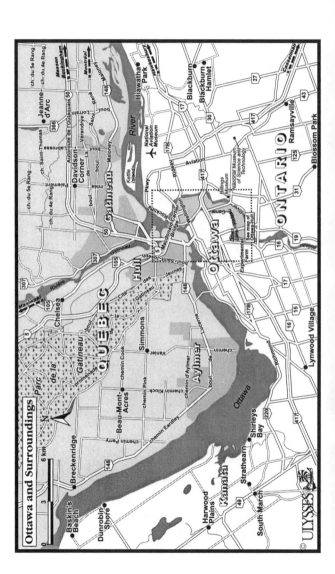

Ottawa and Surroundings

EXPLORING

he Rideau Canal is the heart of Ottawa in two senses. The very foundation of the city was spurred by the construction of the canal, and, geographically, the canal is the dividing line between the eastern part of the city, called Lower Town, and the western part, known as Upper Town. The first tour described in this chapter runs the length of this crucial waterway and presents the main attractions along its shores. The next two tours, Upper Town and Lower Town, reveal the beautiful architectural achievements that transformed Ottawa's image at the turn of the century. Sandy Hill and Along Sussex Drive explore the city's pretty residential neighbourhoods. Finally, a visit to Canada's national capital would not be complete without a jaunt across the Ottawa River to Hull, Québec, Ottawa's sister city. Time permitting, pleasant excursions outside the city are possible; two are proposed, one to the charming hamlet of Merrickville and the other to Upper Canada Village, a fascinating re-creation of a 19th-century settlement.

 TOUR A: THE RIDEAU CANAL ★

Ottawa's existence is in part a result of the British-American War of 1812, in which British authorities realized the extent of the vulnerability of the St. Lawrence River, the vital link between Montreal and the Great Lakes. Once the conflict ended, the British began to devise plans defend the waterway, and they concluded that a canal linking the south bank of the Ottawa River, at the village of Wrightown, to the city of Kingston would provide the security they desired.

Although it made good use of the Rideau and Cataraqui River networks, the Rideau Canal project required great technological prowess on the part of engineers as portions of it as long as 29 kilometres had to be dug. In addition, Colonel By, who was overseeing the work, convinced the authorities to approve a canal not 7.6 metres wide but 15.2 metres wide, so that it could accommodate all sorts of boats and not just military craft. In sum, the scale of the project was enormous for the day. It took six years to complete, and its price was high in both financial and human terms: hundreds of people died of malaria and in accidents during the course of the canal's construction. However with its 47 locks and its 14 dams, the formidable technical achievement that it represents is undeniable.

The canal's impressive entrance, created by Scottish mason Thomas McKay, is still visible from the city. It is made up of eight stone locks that permit boats to descend the first 24.4 metres of the channel. Two mountains overlook the canal, one on either bank. The summit of the eastern hill is now the site of Major's Hill Park (see p 80), but it once bore the stone house of Colonel By, which was destroyed by fire in 1849. The barracks and hospital for the soldiers that built the canal occupied the top of Barrack Hill, on the western shore, until the Parliament Buildings (see p 67) were erected there.

The **Intendance** ★ *($2; mid-May to mid-Jun and Sep to mid-Oct, Mon to Thu 8:30am to 4:30pm, Fri to Sun 8:30am to 7:30pm; mid-Jun to Sep, every day 8:30am to 7:30pm; next to the locks)* was built at the foot of Barrack Hill, just next to the locks, in 1827. This stone house is the oldest edifice in the city and it still encloses the Intendance, in which various exhibitions are mounted.

The Rideau Canal does represent a grandiose project in itself, but it was also a turning point in the nation's history, not only because it was at the root of the founding of Ottawa, but also

The centre of Canadian politics, Ottawa's Parliament Buildings overlook the Rideau Canal. – *P. Quittemelle*

A monument to Canadian peace-keeping forces
in front of the Notre Dame Basilica in Ottawa. – *P. Quittemelle*

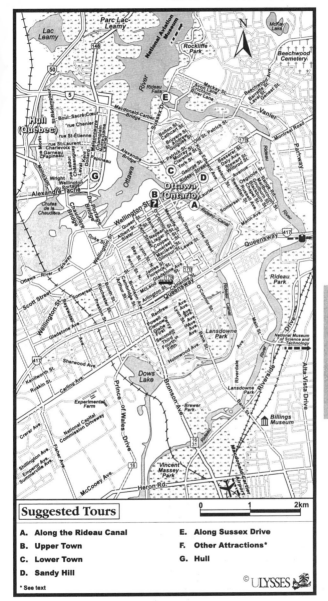

Suggested Tours

A. Along the Rideau Canal

B. Upper Town

C. Lower Town

D. Sandy Hill

E. Along Sussex Drive

F. Other Attractions*

G. Hull

* See text

0   1   2km

© ULYSSES

EXPLORING

because its construction drew numerous workers to the region. particularly masons many of whom were of Scottish origin, who settled in the Rideau River Valley and built the stone houses that are so characteristic of this corner of Ontario. The canal also stimulated the development of commerce in Eastern Ontario, bringing a new level of prosperity to local families.

From very early on beautifying the canal was one of the central preoccupations of developers, so starting at the beginning of the 20th century measures were taken to landscape its shores. Its banks were cleared of debris and a panoramic highway was opened on its western shore.

The **Rideau Canal** snakes through the city, to the great delight of people who come for a breath of fresh air in the urban mélé. In the summer, its banks boast parkland dotted with picnic tables, and there are paths alongside the canal for pedestrians and cyclists. In the winter, once the canal is frozen over, it is transformed into a vast skating rink that crosses the city. There is a small lodge facing the National Arts Centre, where skaters can don their blades and warm up.

The **National Arts Centre** *(between Confederation Square and the Rideau Canal, ☎996-5051)* on the west bank of the canal, occupies the former location of Ottawa's 19th-century city hall, which was destroyed by fire. It was built between 1964 and 1967 by Montreal architects Affleck, Desbarats, Dimakopoulos, Lebensol and Sise. Excellent concerts and plays are presented here throughout the year (see p 138), and the advantages of the centre's canal-side location are amplified in summertime by pleasant patios.

Continue along the canal, either on the Queen Elizabeth Highway on the west bank or on Colonel By Drive on the east bank. If you opt for the latter option and want to reach Dow's Lake Park, take Bronson Avenue, which crosses the canal.

Dows Lake is in a location that was once nothing but swampland. It was artificially created by a dyke and a dam erected during construction of the Rideau Canal. Today this beautiful body of water, situated not too far from downtown Ottawa, is the perfect spot for weekend unwinding: pedal boats, canoes and skates are all available for rent (see p 104), and the lake shore is bordered by a rambling garden that is ideal for picnics and strolls.

TOUR B: UPPER TOWN ★★★

From Bytown's very beginnings, the beautiful west bank of the Rideau Canal was a magnet to the well-to-do English Protestant families who were migrating to the fledgling city. Upper Town, the city's upper-class neighbourhood (if the nascent community could be called a city in those days), became ever more attractive over the years as new houses sprang up to accommodate newly arriving families. The area entered its heyday around the 1860s when Ottawa was chosen as the national capital and the magnificent federal Parliament Buildings were erected on the summit of Barrack Hill, which belonged to the British Crown at the time and which, of course, is still capped by the impressive sight of these government buildings. Within about fifty years, the broad avenues of Upper Town were trimmed with exquisite Victorian buildings by a construction boom in part triggered by the neighbourhood's new prominence.

The half-day tour of this neighbourhood begins at the Parliament Buildings and visits some of the most beautiful buildings in the city.

The **Parliament Buildings ★★★** *(information on activities, ☎239-5000 or 1-800-465-1867)* truly dominate Ottawa. The summit of the hill is topped by three buildings spread over a 200-square-metre garden. Centre Block contains the House of Commons and the Senate, the two chambers of the federal government (see p 68). The two other buildings, East Block and West Block, enclose various administrative offices.

In 1857, when Ottawa was designated the capital of the Province of Canada, city authorities realized that these splendid buildings would have to be built, as there was no appropriate edifice in which to accommodate parliament. A contest was held, and Thomas Fuller and Chilion Jones's plans for a neo-Gothic building won the contract. The deadlines imposed on the designers were very tight and construction began before all of the inevitable kinks in a project of this scale could be worked

EXPLORING

out. The impressive budget of 250,000 pounds sterling that had been allotted for the project was surpassed barely one year later. Authorities were accused of mismanaging public funds, and work on the building was interrupted. Three years passed before a Royal Commission of Inquiry into the affair recommended that construction resume. In 1866, the first session of Parliament was held in the building, which was still unfinished.

Although construction of Centre Block was riddled with problems, the overall project's final result is justifiably the pride of the Ottawa's citizens: three splendid neo-Gothic buildings dominate the horizon of the city, which, up until the erection of the Parliament Buildings, had been a conglomeration of modest wood houses.

At first, Centre Block was comprised of a semi-basement, a ground floor, and only one story. It was topped by a copper mansard roof. At its centre stood Victoria Tower, at a height of 77 metres, which sheltered the entrance. The House of Commons and the Senate were situated in rooms of equal dimensions in either wing of the building. Construction work was finally completed in 1876.

Just 40 years later, on February 3, 1916, a terrible fire broke out in Centre Block, destroying the rooms of the west wing before spreading to those of the east wing. The magnificent edifice was entirely consumed by flame, with the exception of the Library of Parliament, which was spared thanks to the quick wittedness of a clerk who closed the thick iron doors that separated it from the rest of the building. The library, a splendid, 16-sided neo-Gothic building covered by a lantern-shaped roof, may still be visited today. Its interior is richly decorated in white-pine woodwork and comprises a large reading room lit by lancet windows on each of its sides and small alcoves that enclose part of the library collection. Its centre is occupied by a white-marble statue of Queen Victoria that was sculpted by Marshall Wood in 1871.

Reconstruction of Centre Block began some time later and lasted nine years. The architects, John A. Pearson and J. Omer Marchand, designed the new building to be consistent with the East and West Blocks, opting once again for the neo-Gothic style and reproducing the aspect of the original main building.

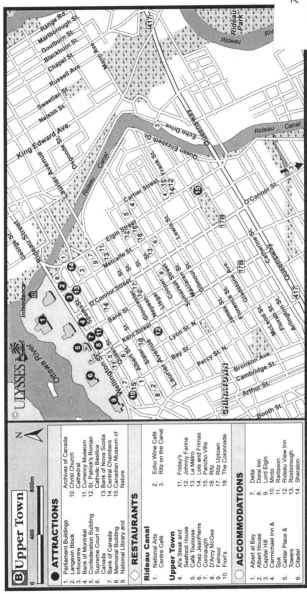

© ULYSSES

B Upper Town

0   400   800m

N

● ATTRACTIONS

1. Parliament Buildings
2. Langevin Block
3. Infocentre
4. Bank of Montréal
5. Confederation Building
6. Supreme Court of Canada
7. Bank of Canada
8. Memorial Building
9. National Library and

10. Archives of Canada
11. Christ Church Cathedral
12. Currency Museum
13. St. Patrick's Roman Catholic Basilica
14. Bank of Nova Scotia
15. Central Chambers
16. Canadian Museum of Nature

◇ RESTAURANTS

Rideau Canal

1. National Arts Centre Café
2. Echo Wine Café
3. Ritz on the Canal

Upper Town

4. Al's Steak and Seafood House
5. Café Toulouse
6. Chez Jean-Pierre
7. Connaught
8. D'Arcy McGee
9. Fairouz
10. Fion's

11. Friday's
12. Johnny Farina
13. Le Métro
14. Lois and Frimas
15. Pancho Villa
16. Ritz
17. Ritz Uptown
18. The Colonnade

ACCOMMODATIONS

1. Albert at Bay
2. Albert House
3. Capital Hill
4. Carmichael Inn & Spa
5. Cartier Place & Towers
6. Citadel

7. Delta
8. Doral Inn
9. Lord Elgin
10. Minto
11. Radisson
12. Rideau View Inn
13. Roxborough
14. Sheraton

EXPLORING

Financial reasons figured in the decision to construct the new building in a style similar to that of its predecessor with like materials. As well, the size of the building had to be reduced; it was later expanded. Its façade is pared by the 90-metre-high Peace Tower which encloses, among other features, a carillon of 53 bells. Nothing, however, was omitted in the decoration of the interior of this splendid building, which incorporates especially magnificent sculptures and woodwork.

Guided tours of Centre Block *(free; late May to early Sep, Mon to Fri 9am to 7:40pm, Sat and Sun 9am to 4:40pm; Sep to May, every day 9am to 4:40pm)* visit the interior of the building, including the west wing where visitors are treated to an up-close look at the House of Commons, in which members of parliament elected through universal suffrage hold debates and adopt federal laws. This vast, rectangular, green-toned room is decorated in white pine, limestone and stained-glass windows depicting the floral emblems of the provinces and territories of Canada.

In the east wing of the building, these guided tours pause at the large room that houses the Senate, the Upper Chamber of the federal administration, whose government-appointed members are responsible for studying and approving laws adopted by the House of Commons. This distinctive room is set apart by carpeting and red armchairs, a coffered ceiling adorned with gold maple leaves and two magnificent and imposing bronze chandeliers.

In addition to these two rooms, the guided tours visit the Library of Parliament as well as the Peace Tower, where you can see the white-marble Memorial Chamber.

Beautiful views of the Ottawa river can be had from the **summer pavilion** on the grounds of Centre Block, behind the building on the west side.

Since the earliest days of its construction, Centre Block has been flanked on either side by East Block and West Block, the work of Thomas Stent and Augustus Laver. East Block, a beautiful composition of asymmetrical elevations, is made of cut stone in shades that range from cream to ochre and is embellished by towers, chimneys, pinnacles, lancet windows, gargoyles and various sculptures. Originally, it was built to house the Canadian civil service; now it encloses the offices of senators and members of Parliament. A guided tour is offered and highlights a few rooms that have been restored to their 19th-century appearances. The Office of the Governor General and the Chamber of the Privy Council are also located here. West Block is used exclusively for the offices of Members of Parliament and is not open to the public.

Parliament is also the scene of numerous events, notably the **changing of the guard**, which takes place every day from late June to late August at 10am, when you can see soldiers parading in their ceremonial garb. A **sound and light show** *(free admission; mid-May to mid-Jun, 9:30pm and 10:30pm)* presents the history of Canada.

On the vast lawn graced with beautiful flowers stretching in front of the parliament buildings, is the centennial flame, inaugurated in 1967 to commemorate the 100th anniversary of Canadian confederation.

When the Parliament Buildings were erected, Wellington Street gained in status, and gradually beautiful buildings sprouted up along it, each rivalling the others in elegance. Among the Second Empire buildings that were erected in that period (this style was very much in fashion in the capital at the end of the 19th century) **Langevin Block** *(facing the Parliament Buildings, Wellington St.)* may still be admired, standing on the spot facing the Parliament Buildings that it has occupied since 1889. Also designed by Thomas Fuller but with a more sober look than that of the Parliament, this building was destined to house government offices. Since 1976, it has been occupied by the Prime Minister's Office.

The large bay windows of the Ottawa tourist information centre, the **Infocentre** *(90 Wellington St.)*, are located two steps away from Langevin Block. A stop here provides a wealth of additional information on accommodations and restaurants in the city, as well as a hotel reservation service.

Stylish Wellington Street has been transformed over the years by new buildings that did not adhere to the neo-Gothic paradigm. At the turn of the 1920s, a branch of the **Bank of Montreal** designed by Ernest I. Barott was unveiled. In keeping with the trend of the era in the architecture of the nation's

EXPLORING

financial institutions, it is pure Art Deco. The stone building has a very simple cubic shape, three sides of which are ornamented with cornices and sculpted with pilasters. The interior is one of the building's crowning glories – it consists of an expansive hall, entirely void of columns and instead elegantly surmounted by a coffered ceiling.

Ottawa's aesthetic face began to take shape at the beginning of the 20th century, as government buildings went up to meet the needs of a growing bureaucracy, most of these influenced by the adoption of a Public Works Department mandate that endorsed the neo-Gothic and Château styles. Wellington Street was the result of the infatuation with these styles and was embellished by cut-stone buildings with pointed roofs, turrets, balconies and dormers. The **Confederation Building** ★, for example, was built next to West Block in about 1928. In the shape of an "L", with an asymmetrical entrance surmounted by a turret with a pointed roof, this building was one of the first projects to combine both of the architectural styles of the day.

Continuing along Wellington Street, another Canadian institution comes into view: the **Supreme Court of Canada** ★ *(corner of Wellington St. and Kent St.)*. This Art Deco building was conceived by architect Ernest Cormier, who began its construction in 1939. Only one modification was brought to its original plans, which called for a flat roof. The Public Works Department, which still favoured the Château style, required that the roof be altered to give it its current appearance (or it may have been requested by Prime Minister Mackenzie King). The tremendous interior space created by this peaked roof is now occupied by the court's library.

Facing the Supreme Court stands the **Bank of Canada**. Its austere-looking light-grey granite façade is a geometric composition minimally enhanced by six pilasters and a coat of arms. A few of its elements were inspired by Greek temples, notably a bronze door engraved with a Greek coin and two urns, symbolizing one of the bank's functions, "to keep the wealth". The original architects had foreseen the extension of this beautiful building in their design; 40 years later a 12-story tower was adjoined to the original building.

The Supreme Court

The Supreme Court was created by the Constitutional Act of 1867 but did not really play the role of final appeal court until 1949. Before then, this function was held by the judiciary committee of the Privy Council in London, a situation that posed complex juridical problems. Despite the fact that Canadian law is inspired by British traditions, there are important distinctions between the two systems. The same building houses the Federal Court of Canada, whose mandate is to settle disputes arising from federal laws.

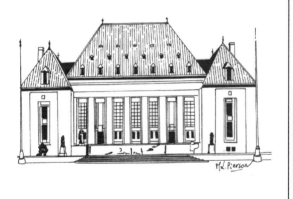

The two edifices that make up the **Memorial Building**, located at the corner of Bank Street, are a more recent interpretation of the Château style, which was in vogue until after the Second World War.

At the end of Wellington Street stand the buildings of the **National Library and Archives of Canada** *(395 Wellington St.)*, which contain an impressive collection of documents dealing with Canada, as well as Canadian publications. Temporary exhibitions are presented here.

EXPLORING

The section of Queen Street between Bay and Bronson is worth a short detour down Bay Street to see its beautiful turn-of-the-century homes.

Three magnificent Queen Anne houses stand at numbers 406-408 and 410. Covered in red brick and ornamented with gables, stained-glass windows and balconies, they are a good indication of what the streets of the city might have looked like at the turn of the century.

Across the street, beautiful **Christ Church Cathedral** *(439 Queen St.)* has been renowned for the resplendence of its choir since its inauguration in 1932.

Queen Street offers little else of interest. A series of high-rises sprouted up in the years around 1965, when the law that proscribed buildings taller than the Parliament was revoked. Businessman Jean Campeau took advantage of this relaxation of restrictions to erect **Place de Ville**, a tall black monolith. Following this lead, many office towers were built in this part of the city. As these are of no particular charm, backtrack to Sparks Street.

The considerable changes that Ottawa underwent in the second half of the 19th century had repercussions on the development of its commercial arteries. From the town's very beginnings, two sections of it have vied for the status of business centre: the surroundings of the Byward Market, in Lower Town, and **Sparks Street**, in Upper Town. Great effort was expended by local residents and shopkeepers to embellish Sparks Street and, thanks to them, this elegant road of five- and six-story buildings was one of the very first to be paved with asphalt, to have streetcar service and to be illuminated by street lamps. In those days it was known as the "Broadway" of Ottawa. Its commercial role never ebbed, and today it offers a beautiful pedestrian mall between Kent and Elgin Streets that is especially pleasant in the summertime when its concentration of pretty shops attracts crowds of patrons and browsers.

The first stop on Sparks Street is a visit to the **Currency Museum** ★ *($2; Tue to Sat 10:30am to 5pm, Sun 1pm to 5pm; 245 Sparks St., ☎782-8914)*, which is located inside the Bank of Canada, by the rear entrance. The exhibition is spread over eight rooms and retraces the history of the creation of currency. The first room deals with the first objects that served as trading tender: natives used wampum "belts" adorned with shell beads. From there the exhibition traces the evolution of the coin from China, where it had its earliest use, to Florence, where coins were made out of precious metals for the first time (the florin). Rooms three through six cover the development of Canadian currency from the exchange of glassware for beaver pelts to French colonists' use of playing cards as bills of exchange while they waited money to arrive from France, to the creation of Canadian paper currency. Numismatists will be interested in room eight, which displays a beautiful collection of antique coins and bills. Finally, there is a short educational film about the role of the Bank of Canada.

If you have a little extra time, make a detour down Kent Street to Nepean Street to see **Saint Patrick's Roman Catholic Basilica** ★ *(281 Nepean St.)*, which serves the oldest English-speaking Catholic parish in Ottawa. This long stone building surmounted by a bell tower was finished in 1875. Inside, you can admire its beautiful neo-Gothic interior adorned with stained-glass windows and a Casavant organ.

Backtrack to and continue along Sparks Street.

At number 118 is another branch of a large Canadian bank, the **Bank of Nova Scotia** ★. Erected in 1923-24, this Art-Deco building is complemented by a beautiful façade supported by four Doric columns. Above the columns, the building culminates with a frieze of motifs representing prosperity and Canadian history.

Continue to Elgin Street.

The **Central Chambers Building** ★, at the corner of Elgin and Queen, is a good example of the late 19th-century architecture of commercial buildings. Professionals, particularly lawyers, rented office space here, launching the trend that made this neighbourhood so popular. The building was renovated in the early 1980s in a project that preserved its magnificent oblique façade of huge windows, the last row of which, on the fifth floor, is gabled. The ground floor is still occupied by shops.

Either continue along Elgin Street – explore its pretty shops or take a break at one of its many restaurants – or, for a longer

EXPLORING

tour, turn right on McLoed Street to visit the Canadian Nature Museum.

The **Canadian Museum of Nature** ★ *($4; May to Sep, every day 9:30am to 5pm, Thu to 8pm; Sep to May, every day 10am to 5pm, Thu to 8pm; corner of McLoed St. and Metcalfe St., ☎566-4700)*, in a huge, recently renovated three-story building, houses many small exhibitions on various facets of nature. Myriad themes, including geology, the formation of the planet, animals of prehistoric Canada, indigenous mammals and birds of Canada, and the fantastic world of insects and of vegetable life, are presented in an interesting manner.

 TOUR C: LOWER TOWN ★★★

In the early days of Bytown, the poorly irrigated land on the east bank of the canal was unappealing to newcomers. Irrigation work was carried out in 1827, making it more attractive, and gradually it was populated, but not by the well-to-do. Labourers looking for affordable housing established themselves here, and French and Irish workers, most of them Catholic, made up the majority in this neighbourhood. Conditions were difficult; skirmishes between the Irish and the French, who were often competing for the same jobs, were frequent; and life in the neighbourhood was not always rosy. Few traces remain of these first difficult years in Lower Town, as the buildings of the era, most of which were made of wood, rarely resisted the wear of the years. A few of these scattered here and there mostly reflect the French origins of neighbourhood residents. Left by the wayside in the second half of the 19th century, the neighbourhood was left out of the building boom that overtook Upper Town. Here, there are very few of the neo-Gothic constructions that were so popular in that period. At the beginning of the 20th century, Sussex Drive, which delimits the western edge of the neighbourhood, was embellished by the construction of magnificent Château-style buildings. Then, over the course of this century, other buildings, including the very beautiful National Gallery of Canada, perfected the image of this elegant artery.

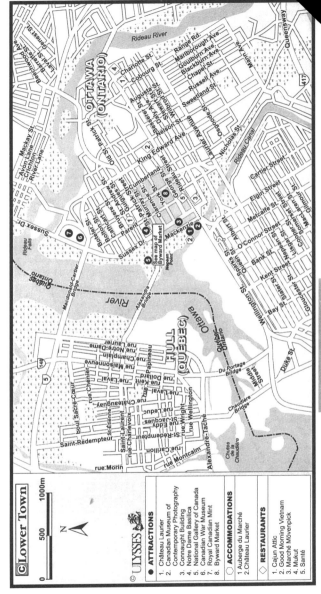

© ULYSSES

CLower Town

0   500   1000m

N

● ATTRACTIONS

1. Château Laurier
2. Canadian Museum of Contemporary Photography
3. Connaught Building
4. Notre Dame Basilica
5. National Gallery of Canada
6. Canadian War Museum
7. Royal Canadian Mint
8. Byward Market

○ ACCOMMODATIONS

1. Auberge du Marché
2. Château Laurier

◇ RESTAURANTS

1. Cajun Attic
2. Good Morning Vietnam
3. Marché Mövenpick
4. Mukut
5. Santé

EXPLORING

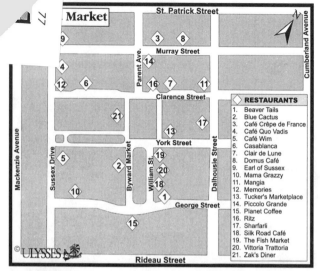

Market

Murray Street

Clarence Street

York Street

George Street

Rideau Street

Parent Ave.

Byward Market

William St.

Dalhousie Street

Mackenzie Avenue

Sussex Drive

Cumberland Avenue

©ULYSSES

RESTAURANTS
1. Beaver Tails
2. Blue Cactus
3. Café Crêpe de France
4. Café Quo Vadis
5. Café Wim
6. Casablanca
7. Clair de Lune
8. Domus Café
9. Earl of Sussex
10. Mama Grazzy
11. Mangia
12. Memories
13. Tucker's Marketplace
14. Piccolo Grande
15. Planet Coffee
16. Ritz
17. Sharfarli
18. Silk Road Café
19. The Fish Market
20. Vittoria Trattoria
21. Zak's Diner

Wellington Street spans the canal, becoming Rideau Street on this bank, where it is lined with a multitude of shops that are fun to browse through a spell.

The first building on the tour is the unmistakable and imposing **Château Laurier ★ ★** *(1 Rideau St.)*, on the shore of the Rideau Canal, which has been one of the most prestigious hotels in the city since the day it opened its doors (see p 113).

The Château Laurier's origins are intrinsically linked to the construction of the cross-Canada Grand Trunk Railroad. Cornelius Van Horne, then the head of the Canadian Pacific Railway Company, realized that he needed to increase the number of passengers on this track to make it turn a profit so he decided to establish a coast-to-coast chain of prestigious hotels along the route. The first of these establishments to be erected was the Château Frontenac in Quebec City, but the nation's capital would not be outdone: about 15 years later the company contracted Bradford Lee Gilbert to design Ottawa's luxury hotel. Gilbert was let go before construction could begin, so architects Ross and MacFarland were hired in 1908 to complete the blueprints. They favoured the Château style, to keep with the look of the other Canadian Pacific hotels, and built an elegant, romantically alluring hotel of relatively bare

Château Laurier

stone façades topped by pointed copper roofs, turrets and dormers. No detail was overlooked in making this a hotel of the highest quality, and the interior decoration, which can be admired in the lobby, is sumptuous. The very first guest to register, in 1912, was none other than Sir Wilfrid Laurier, who had strongly supported the creation of the railroad and in whose honour the hotel was named.

Next to this is the **Canadian Museum of Contemporary Photography** *(free admission; May to Sep, Mon and Tue, Fri and Sun 11am to 5pm, Wed 4pm to 8pm, Thu 11am to 8pm; Sep to Apr, Wed and Thu 11am to 8pm, Fri to Sun 11am to 5pm; 1 Rideau Canal, ☎993-4497)*, with a collection containing more than 158,000 images created from the photographic resources of the National Film Board of Canada.

Continue on Mackenzie Avenue.

Faithful to the architectural tradition that prevailed in the capital at the beginning of the century, the **Connaught Building** ★, erected in 1913-1914, is pure neo-Gothic. Architect David Ewart was inspired by many English buildings of the Tudor era, particularly Hampton Court and Windsor Castle, in the conception of these plans. The building boasts crenellated turrets at each end and at its centre.

Major's Hill rises at the mouth of the Rideau Canal, on the east bank. This land which borders the entrance to the canal and the Ottawa River, belonged for a long time to the British Crown, which, when Bytown was founded, had decided to keep it in order to ensure the protection of the canal. The only building erected on its summit was the residence of Colonel By, but it was destroyed by fire in 1849. In 1864, in a project to beautify the city, the land was transformed into a huge park – the city's very first – **Major's Hill Park**. Stretched along the Ottawa River, it remains one of the city's most beautiful green spaces. It envelops **Nepean Point**, which juts into the river and which offers a lovely view of the Parliament Buildings. The Astrolabe Theatre, where various events are organized in summer, is also within the park confines.

Turn right onto St. Patrick Street.

In 1841, **Notre Dame Basilica** ★★ *(Sussex Dr. at the corner of Saint Patrick St.)*, topped by two elegant steeples, was built to serve Catholics in Lower Town, French-speakers as well as the English-speaking Irish. In the choir stall, you will notice the presence of Saint John the Baptist and of Saint Patrick. This is the oldest church in the city. Its magnificent choir stall of finely worked wood and statues of the prophets and evangelists by Louis-Philippe Hébert are still in perfect condition.

Continue along Sussex Drive.

The **National Gallery of Canada** ★★★ *(free admission to the permanent collection; Jun to early Oct, every day 10am to 6pm; Oct to late May, Wed to Sun 10am to 5pm, Tue 10am to 8pm; 380 Sussex Dr., ☎990-1985)*, with its collection of 45,000 works of art, 1,200 of which are on display, offers a fabulous trip through the art history of Canada and elsewhere. Rising above the Ottawa River, this modern glass, granite and concrete building, a masterpiece by architect Moshe Safdie, is

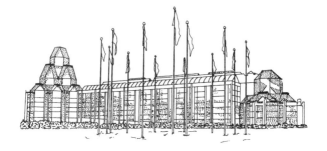

National Gallery

easily identified by its harmonious tower, covered with glass triangles, recalling the shape of the parliamentary library visible in the distance.

Once inside, the museum seems to draw you. You'll first walk up the Colonnnade, stopping for a minute to contemplate the Boreal Garden outside, inspired by the work of the Group of Seven. Once in the Grand Hall, the spectacular view of the Parliament Buildings and the Ottawa River unfolds before you.

The first rooms of the museum, on the ground floor, are devoted to the works of Canadian and American artists. Fifteen of these rooms trace the evolution of Canadian artistic movements. Some of the finest canvasses from the 19th century are exhibited there, notably *Sister Saint Alphonse* by Antoine Plamondon, recognized as one of the earliest Canadian masterpieces. You can also see works by Cornelius Krieghoff, an artist of Dutch descent who portrayed the lives of ordinary people in the early days of colonization with great brio.

The following rooms present important works by artists who made their mark in the early 20th century. Among them, are canvasses by the Ontario painter Tom Thomson (*The Jack Pine)* and by members of the Group of Seven (including *The Red Maple* by A.Y. Jackson), who created unique works in the modern interpretation of natural scenes from the Canadian Shield. Space is also given to artists who gained renown by creating painting techniques and exploiting themes that were particular to them, including British Columbian artist Emily Carr

EXPLORING

(*Indian Hut, Queen Charlotte Islands*). You can also contemplate canvasses by great 20th-century Québec painters, notably Alfred Pellan (*On the Beach*), Jean-Paul Riopelle (*Pavane*), Jean-Paul Lemieux (*The Visit*), and Paul-Émile Borduas (*Leeward of the Island).*

The Group of Seven

In the early years of the 20th century, some of the great Ontario landscape painters became known by creating genuinely Canadian art. **Tom Thomson**, whose paintings provide a distinctive portrayal of landscapes unique to the Canadian Shield, was an originator of this movement. He died prematurely in 1917 at the age of 40, though his work had an indisputable effect over one of the most notable groups of painters in Ontario, the **Group of Seven**, whose first exhibition was held in Toronto in 1920. These artists, **Franklin Carmichael, Lawren S. Harris, Frank H. Johnson, Arthur Lismer, J.E.H. MacDonald, Alexander Young Jackson** and **Frederick Varley**, were all landscape painters. Although they worked together closely, each developed his own pictorial language. They were distinguished by their use of bright colours in their portrayal of typical Canadian landscapes. Their influence over Ontario painting is substantial.

The ground floor also includes Inuit art galleries, which are worthy of special attention. With about 160 sculptures and 200 prints, they provide an occasion to admire several masterpieces of Inuit art. Among them, *The Enchanted Owl* by Kenojuak and the beautiful sculpture *Man and Woman Seated with a Child*.

The museum also houses an impressive collection of American and European works. Works of the great masters are presented in chronological order, and in the course of your visit you can contemplate creations by famous painters such as the Pierre-Paul Rubens work *The Entombment*. The rooms containing 19th-century canvasses present several surprises, including *Mercury and Argus* by Turner, *Woman and Umbrella* by Edgar Degas, *Waterloo Bridge: The Sun in the Fog* by Claude Monet, *Forest* by Paul Cézanne, and *Hope I* by Gustav Klimt. The achievements of 20th-century artists are also highlighted; the museum exhibits canvasses including *Nude on Yellow Sofa* by Matisse, *The Small Table* by Picasso, *The Glass of Absinth* by Georges Braque, *Number 29* by Jackson Pollock, and *In the Line of Fire* by Barnett Newman. The collection of American artincludes several lithographies by Roy Lichtenstein and Andy Warhol.

The string of rooms on the ground floor surrounds a very unique gallery that houses an under-appreciated work: the beautiful interior of the **Chapelle du Couvent Notre-Dame-du-Sacré-Coeur**, designed by Georges Bouillon in 1887-1888. When the convent was demolished in 1972, the structure of the chapel was taken apart piece by piece and preserved. A few years later, a room was specially laid out in the National Gallery to accommodate it. Its splendid choir and its wooden, fan-shaped vaults and cast-iron columns may still be admired here.

Museum lovers can continue along Sussex Drive to the Canadian War Museum and the Royal Canadian Mint.

The entrance to the **Canadian War Museum ★** *($3.50; May to mid-Oct, every day 9:30am to 5pm, Thu to 8pm; mid-Oct to May, closed Mon; 330 Sussex Dr., ☎776-8627)* is impossible to miss, what with a tank sitting on the lawn in front of it. The museum was laid out in a beautiful building designed at the beginning of the century by David Ewart to house the National Archives. The exhibitions are spread over three stories and retrace the history of the Canadian Army from its very first battles in the early days of colonization to its participation in the great world events that have marked the 20th century. Weapons, uniforms and medals of the French military, from the very earliest stages of colonization, and of the British army, which came next, are exposed on the ground floor. These various objects, in addition to their interest in themselves, are used to relate some of the major events of the colonial wars. On the second floor, the Canadian army's involvement in the WW II is recounted through short films, models, weapons of all sorts, uniforms and other objects. Finally, on the top story, there is an exhibition that highlights the role of peacekeepers.

Just next door to the Canadian War Museum is the building that houses the **Royal Canadian Mint ★** *($2; Mon to Fri 9am to*

EXPLORING

4pm, Sat and Sun 10am to 5pm; 320 Sussex Dr., ☎993-8990), the plans of which were conceived by Ewart in 1905-1908. Common Canadian coins were once struck here, but today the mint produces only silver, gold and platinum collector's pieces. The entire process may be seen here: the selection and.cutting of precious metals, the striking of the coins and the quality control procedure. It is best to visit during the week when it is possible to see the coins being made through large bay windows; tours are offered on the weekend, but in the absence of workers the whole process has to be imagined.

Backtrack to Clarence Street and turn left. Turn right onto Byward and proceed to the Byward Market.

One of Ottawa's liveliest places, the **Byward Market** ★★ *(around York and George streets)* is a pleasant open-air market where various merchants assemble to sell fruits, vegetables, flowers and all sorts of other treasures and knick-knacks. All around, and on the neighbouring streets, there are many shops, restaurants, bars and cafés, some of them with pretty outdoor terraces. On fine summer days, the area is at its most lively, with crowds of people out for a stroll or a little shopping.

On sunny summer days, the market is bustling with relaxed crowds strolling around and shoppers seeking out special ingredients.

 TOUR D: SANDY HILL

In Bytown's earliest days, the city developed in two sections, Upper Town and Lower Town. The designation of Ottawa as Canada's national capital led to profound changes as the city underwent major growth: myriad buildings went up to meet the needs of newcomers. Around the 1870s, a new class began to emerge, made up of bureaucrats and federal government representatives, all of whom would have to live in the capital. These people earned comfortable incomes for their efforts and moved into a new neighbourhood called Sandy Hill, between Rideau and Mann Streets, on land that until then had been the undivided property of Louis Besserer. This area of the city, comprised of beautiful homes and lush gardens, remains one of Ottawa's most pleasant.

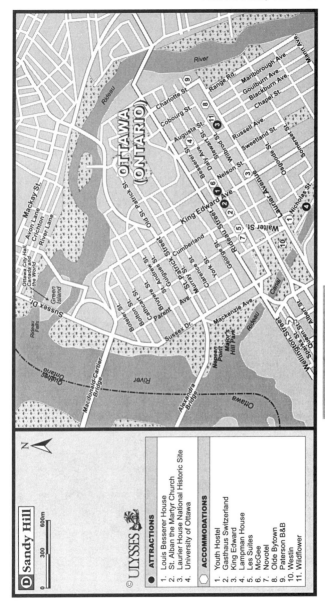

© ULYSSES

ⓓ Sandy Hill

0   300   600m

N

ATTRACTIONS

1. Louis Besserer House
2. St. Alban the Martyr Church
3. Laurier House National Historic Site
4. University of Ottawa

ACCOMMODATIONS

1. Youth Hostel
2. Gasthaus Switzerland
3. King Edward
4. Les Suites
5. McGee
6. Novotel
7. Olde Bytown
8. Paterson B&B
9. Westin
10. Wildflower

EXPLORING

Take Rideau Street to King Edward Avenue and turn right.

At the corner of Daly Street and King Edward Avenue there is a Georgian house of cut stone that dates from 1844. Built well before the area became fashionable, this home belonged to Louis Besserer, who owned all of the land that would become the neighbourhood known first as the St. George Ward and later as Sandy Hill.

St. Alban the Martyr, a cut-stone church that dates from 1867, is just across King Edward Avenue. Construction of this neo-Gothic church was begun by Fuller, the architect credited with the Central Block of the Parliament, and finished by King Arnoldi. Today it is the oldest still-standing Protestant church in the city.

Continue east on Daly Street, a thoroughfare that is especially interesting to architecture buffs because it is lined with buildings reflecting a variety of styles including beautiful upper-class residences side by side with working-class homes.

The red-brick McFarlane row houses that stand at number 201 constitute one of the area's earliest developments (1868).

Among the pretty houses on the street that date from the last century, one that stands out is Winterholme House (at 309-311), a stone house with a wood-shingle roof that was built for the Queens Printer.

Continuing along Daly there are more beautiful examples of the architecture of the late 19th century. Turn right on Charlotte Street, then left on Wilbrod.

Paterson House, designed by architect J. W. H. Watts between 1901 and 1903, sits at 500 Wilbrod Street. This pretty Queen Anne house has not lost any of its charm with age; in 1992 it was impeccably renovated and converted into a bed and breakfast (see p 112).

Strathcona Park sprawls along the Rideau River at the end of Charlotte Street, providing a beautiful green space and an ideal spot for a short rest.

Turn right on Laurier Avenue.

Laurier House ★ *($2.25; Apr to Sep, Tue to Sat 9am to 5pm, Sun 2pm to 5pm; Oct to Mar, Tue to Sat 10am to 5pm, Sun 2pm to 5pm; 335 Laurier Ave. E., ☎692-2581)*, a delightful residence built in 1878, belonged to Sir Wilfrid Laurier. He was elected Prime Minister of Canada in 1896, and that year his party, the Liberal Party of Canada, offered him this house. Laurier was the first French-speaker to become Canadian Prime Minister, a post he held until 1911; he lived in this house until his death in 1919. Later, Lady Laurier gave it to William Lyon Mackenzie King, who succeeded her husband as Liberal leader. When King died in 1950, the house was bequeathed to the government as part of Canada's heritage. Visiting it today, you can explore several rooms decorated according to King's tastes and a few others decorated with the Laurier family's furniture.

Ottawa University, previously known as Ottawa College, was originally run by a religious order and served the Catholic communities of Ottawa. Now the university is a renowned educational institution. Its campus is bordered by Laurier Avenue, Nicholas Street and King Edward Avenue.

The end of Laurier Avenue abuts the Rideau Canal.

The Ottawa Congress Centre, located on the shore of the canal, hosts various events throughout the year.

 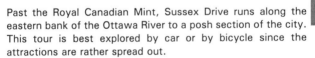

TOUR E: ALONG SUSSEX DRIVE ★★

Past the Royal Canadian Mint, Sussex Drive runs along the eastern bank of the Ottawa River to a posh section of the city. This tour is best explored by car or by bicycle since the attractions are rather spread out.

First stop is **Earnscliffe**, a superb neo-Gothic residence overlooking the Ottawa River that dates from 1856-1857. It was originally home to the family of John MacKinnon, son-in-law of Thomas McKay, who designed the entrance to the Rideau Canal. A few years after MacKinnon's death in 1870, Prime Minister John A. Macdonald was a tenant here. He bought the house about 10 years later and lived out the rest of his years in it. Today Earnscliffe is home to the British High Commission.

EXPLORING

At Green Island the Rideau River empties into the Ottawa in two pretty waterfalls that form a curtain (hence the river's name; *rideau* is French for "curtain"). Take a moment to stop at the belvedere at the top of the falls; it offers a magnificent **view** ★ of the river and of the city in the distance.

Ottawa City Hall ★ stands on Green Island, and its modern look was the pride of the city in 1958 when it was inaugurated. Over the years the city administration outgrew this stone, aluminum and glass building, and, to preserve it, it was expanded rather than replaced. Moshe Safdie, the architect of the National Gallery of Canada (see p 80), was commissioned to oversee the work.

The **Canada and the World** interpretive centre *(free; early Jun to early Sep, every day; rest of the year, weekends only)* is also located on the island. It presents an exhibition that explains Canada's role in other countries.

A series of magnificent homes appears next, but number 24 should catch your eye. It is an immense stone house surrounded by a beautiful garden – the **Official Residence of the Prime Minister of Canada**. Built in 1867 for businessman Joseph Currier, it became the home of Canadian prime ministers in 1949. For obvious reasons it is not open to the public.

Not far from 24 Sussex Drive another splendid residence crops up, surrounded by a pleasant and huge garden that covers 40 hectares: **Rideau Hall** ★★ *(free; schedule varies; 1 Sussex Dr., ☎998-7113)*. This is the official residence of Canada's Governor General, the representative of the Queen of England, Elizabeth II. It is a sumptuous Regency-style home that was built in 1838 for Thomas McKay, the designer of the entrance to the Rideau Canal (see p 64). In 1865, the government rented the building to accommodate the governor general of the day, Lord Monck, and then bought the property in 1868. Since then, many modifications have been made to the original building, which has been in continual use as an official residence.

A vast and pleasant garden surrounds the house, where you can linger about. Guided tours are offered during the summer of the five rooms open to the public.

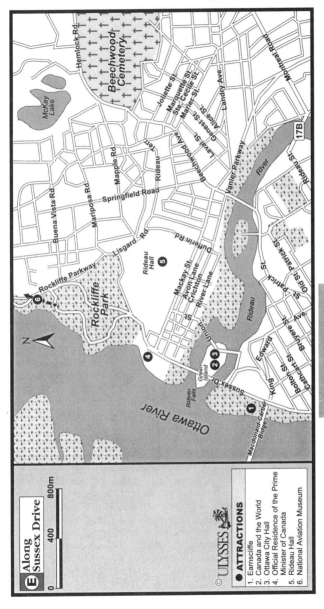

© ULYSSES

● ATTRACTIONS

1. Earnscliffe
2. Canada and the World
3. Ottawa City Hall
4. Official Residence of the Prime Minister of Canada
5. Rideau Hall
6. National Aviation Museum

E Along Sussex Drive

0   400   800m

Take the time to stroll along the streets in the area of Rideau Hall and see the area's beautiful houses, some of which have been converted into embassies.

Facing Rideau Hall is a lovely green space, **Rockliffe Park**, with lookouts offering fine views of Hull and the Gatineau River.

Past the park, Sussex Drive becomes Rockliffe Drive.

Visitors are immediately impressed upon entering the **National Aviation Museum ★★★** *($5; May to Sep, every day 9am to 5pm, Thu to 8pm; Sep to May, Tue to Sun 10am to 5pm; Rockliffe Airport, ☎993-2010)* by the unique atmosphere of this huge, wonderfully laid-out building. The fascinating exhibition housed here and culled from the museum's beautiful collection of airplanes thoroughly brings to light the dazzling, rapid-fire evolution that so far is just one-hundred-years long. Eight themes are developped: the era of pioneers, the First World War, bush piloting, airlines, the British Commonwealth training plan, the Second World War, air and sea forces, and the era of jet planes. Among the 45 planes displayed in the interior of the museum (seven planes are exhibited outside and there are even more in a storage area that sometimes figures on the guided tour), some are particularly captivating. An exhibit features models of wood and canvas planes that were the first ever to take to the air, and a short film relates the exploits of the first brave pilots to ride these flying engines. The Curtiss HS-2L and the sturdy Beaver are used to illustrate the importance of commercial flying in the exploration of Canada's immense territory. Planes that became famous in the Second World War, such as the Avro Lancaster bomber, the Hawker Hurricane fighter and the Messerschmitt, a German-designed jet, are highlighted. Finally, a few jets are displayed, including the Lockheed F-104A Starfighter. The appeal of this museum, aside from the airplanes, lies in the great story of aviation that it retells through reconstructions and consistently clear explanations of both technical and historical aspects. Interactive exhibitions – particularly "Full Flight", which uses games to explain the basic principals of aerodynamics – along with films and demonstrations, including the very popular "Lighter than Air", aim to familiarize young people and the young-at-heart with the aeronautical world. An audio tour may be rented *($2)*.

TOUR F: OTHER ATTRACTIONS

Ottawa has a few other sights worth visiting that, although not far, are located outside the city centre and not within the confines of any tour described above.

From downtown take Rideau Street, which becomes Montreal Road past Cummings Bridge, to St. Laurent Boulevard, which leads to the National Museum of Science and Technology.

The **National Museum of Science and Technology** ★★ *($6; May to Sep, every day 9am to 6pm, Fri to 9pm; Sep to Apr, Tue to Sun 9am to 5pm; 1867 St. Laurent Blvd., ☎991-3044)* offers a pleasant opportunity to enter the world of science and technology – a universe that may seem too complex at first glance to some. The appeal of this museum is not based on any particular exhibition but rather on its panoply of interactive presentations on various subjects. For example, computer science is tackled in an exhibition entitled "Connexions": about 500 computers are displayed, illustrating the extraordinary technological leaps and bounds that the field has made in just 50 years. Another exhibition, "Love, Leisure and Laundry", recounts the evolution of the multitude of little tools used in our daily lives – like lamps, toilets and iceboxes – that have greatly contributed to our improved standard of living. Other fascinating topics are also dealt with, such as transportation and printing. Through games, explanatory panels and models of all sorts, visitors to the museum gain a better understanding of how the world works and have fun at the same time.

From downtown take Queen Elizabeth Drive, then Bank Street to Riverside Drive, then Pleasant Park Road to the intersection of Cabot Street.

The Billings family were among the first colonists to settle in Bytown. In 1827-1828 a beautiful neoclassical home was built for them; it has survived all these years and now houses the **Billings Estate Museum** *($2.50; May to Oct, Sun to Thu noon to 5pm; 2100 Cabot St., ☎247-4830)*. Furniture, photographs and various curios are exhibited, illustrating daily life in the early days of the city, and guides make the museum even more

EXPLORING

pleasant. A large garden of flowers and trees surrounds the building.

From downtown take Queen Elizabeth Drive, which becomes Prince of Wales Drive.

The **Central Experimental Farm** *(Prince of Wales Drive, ☎995-5222)* is surrounded by a vast garden adorned with lovely flowers in the summer. It includes an arboretum where nearly 2,000 species of trees are grown. You can also see animals, including dairy cows, beef cattle, horses and sheep. As well, an agriculture museum presents different types of farm machinery used throughout the 20th century.

Three Ottawa Neighbourhoods

Somerset Street is a long thoroughfare lined with charming shops and restaurants that crosses the southern part of Upper Town from east to west. The first little nexus of businesses is in the vicinity of Bank Street. Going west, strollers come upon another facet of the capital: **Chinatown**. Although it is not as large as those of Montreal or Toronto, Ottawa's Chinatown does cover a few blocks between Bronson and Booth. It has a flurry of storefronts filled with a thousand and one Chinese products, shops fragranced by Oriental spices and restaurants with menus of Dim Sum and Cantonese specialties.

East of Bank Street, Somerset intersects Preston Avenue, a north-south artery that fostered the development of another very pleasant ethnic neighbourhood, **Little Italy**. Although to some this neighbourhood might seem less exotic than Chinatown, it does conceal a few gratifying finds, including fine grocery stores and family restaurants that serve incomparable cuisine.

Finally, the **Glebe**, which extends out from Bank Street south of Queensway, is a lively, stylish neighbourhood of chic boutiques and fine restaurants where the urge to wander about, eye's wide at the sight of pretty houses, is very compelling. This peaceful residential area is ideal for sunny-day strolls.

TOUR G: HULL, QUÉBEC ★

The Du Portage Bridge crosses the Ottawa River over Victoria Island, leading from Ottawa to Hull. The area at the foot of the bridge on the Ottawa side of the river was once known as Lebreton Flats, and an industrial district developed there in proximity to the sawmills. Until the decline of the lumber industry in the 20th century, piles of wood cluttered the banks of the river, but today the only traces of this era that remain are the defunct mills on Victoria Island.

Although the road leading into Hull is named after an important post-war town planner, the city is certainly not a model of enlightened urban development. It's architecture is very unlike that of Ottawa, just across the river. The town was founded in 1800 by American Loyalist Philemon Wright who was involved in agriculture and the exploitation of the Ottawa valley's rich virgin forests. In 1850, Hull became an important wood-processing centre. For many generations the Eddy Company, which is based in the area, has been supplying matches to the entire world.

The modest wood-frame houses that line the streets of Hull are nicknamed "matchboxes" because they once housed many employees of the Eddy match factory, and because they have had more than their fair share of fires. In fact, Hull has burned so many times throughout its history that few of the town's historical buildings remain. The former town hall and beautiful Catholic church burned down in 1971 and 1972, respectively. Ottawa has the reputation of being a quiet city, while Hull is considered more of a fun town, essentially because Québec laws are more lenient.

Turn left onto Rue Papineau. The parking lot of the Musée Canadien des Civilisations is at the end of this street.

EXPLORING

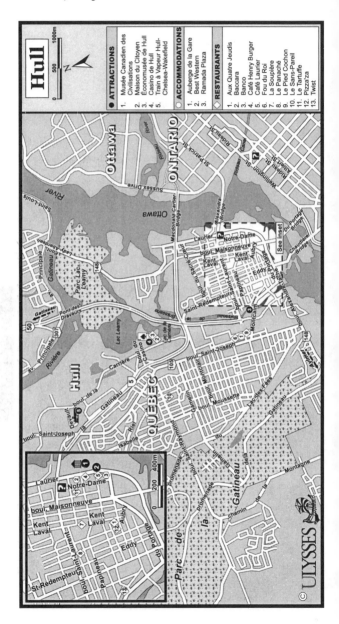

Hull

0   500   1000m

● **ATTRACTIONS**

1. Musée Canadien des Civilisations
2. Maison du Citoyen
3. Éconumusée de Hull
4. Casino de Hull
5. Train à Vapeur Hull-Chelsea-Wakefield

○ **ACCOMMODATIONS**

1. Auberge de la Gare
2. Best Western
3. Ramada Plaza

◇ **RESTAURANTS**

1. Aux Quatre Jeudis
2. Baccara
3. Banco
4. Café Henry Burger
5. Café Laurier
6. Fou du Roi
7. La Soupière
8. Le Panaché
9. Le Pied Cochon
10. Le Sans-Pareil
11. Le Tartuffe
12. Pizza'za
13. Twist

© ULYSSES

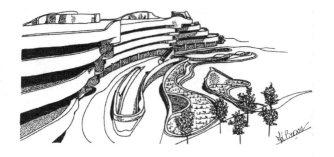

Musée Canadien des Civilisations

The **Musée Canadien des Civilisations** ★★★ *($5, free admission on Sun 9am to noon; May to mid-Oct, every day 9am to 6pm; mid-Oct to late Apr, every day 9am to 5pm; Jul to Sep, Fri to 9pm; Thu until 9pm all year; 100 Rue Laurier, ☎776-7000).* Many parks and museums were established along this section of the Québec-Ontario border as part of a large redevelopment program in the National Capital Region between 1983 and 1989. Hull became the site of the magnificent Musée Canadien des Civilisations, dedicated to the history of Canada's various cultural groups. If there is one museum that must be seen in Canada it is this one. Douglas Cardinal of Alberta drew up the plans for the museum's two striking curved buildings, one housing the administrative offices and restoration laboratories, and the other the museum's collections. Their undulating design brings to mind rock formations of the Canadian Shield, shaped by wind and glaciers. There is a beautiful view of Ottawa River and Parliament Hill from the grounds behind the museum.

The Grande Gallerie (Great Hall) houses the most extensive collection of native totem poles in the world. Another collection brilliantly recreates different periods in Canadian history, from the arrival of the Vikings around 1000 AD to life in rural Ontario in the 19th century and French Acadia in the 17th century. Contemporary native art, as well as popular arts and traditional crafts are also on display. In the Musée des Enfants (Children's Museum), young visitors choose a theme before being led through an extraordinary adventure. Screening rooms are

EXPLORING

equipped with OMNIMAX technology, a new system developed by the creators of the large-screen IMAX. Most of the movies shown here deal with Canadian geography.

Continue south on Rue Laurier. At Rue Montcalm, turn right.
The mission of the **Écomusée de Hull** *($5; Apr to Oct 10am to 6pm, Nov to Mar 10am to 4pm; Rue Montcalm, ☎595-7790)* is to make people more aware of ecological issues, and to achieve this goal, it presents various exhibits on themes such as the origin of the solar system and the evolution of planet Earth. This institution, however, goes beyond tracing the origins of life on earth, because it is also home to an insectarium with no less than 4,000 different species of insects. Finally, you can also take a look at a small exhibit on the industrial history of the city.

Take Highway 50, then Highway 5 north to the Boulevard du Casino exit. Then take Rue Saint-Raymond, which becomes Boulevard du Casino.

The **Casino de Hull** ★ ★ *(11am to 3am; 1 Boulevard du Casino, ☎1-800-665-2274 or 772-2100)* has an impressive location between two lakes; Leamy Lake, in the park of the same name, and Lac de la Carrière, which is in the basin of an old limestone quarry. The theme of water is omnipresent all around the superb building, inaugurated in 1996. The magnificent walkway leading to the main entrance is dotted with towering fountains, and the harbour has 20 slips for boaters. The gambling area, which is 2,741 square metres in size, includes 1,300 slot machines and 58 playing tables spread around a simulated tropical forest. Quebec painter Jean-Paul Riopelle's famous 40-metre-long painting, **Hommage à Rosa Luxembourg**, dominates the room. The artist created this immense triptych in honour of Joan Mitchell, his partner of many years. The opening of the casino also marked the first annual fireworks festival, **Les Grands Feux du Casino** *(☎771-FEUX or 800-771-FEUX)*, which takes place every year in August. The casino has excellent restaurants, including Baccara (see p 132), and two bars. The casino opened a heliport in 1997.

Continue driving south of the Ottawa River. Take Boulevard de la Carrière to Rue Deveault.

The magnificent glass tower of the National Gallery of Canada, a masterpiece by architect Moshe Safdie. – *Neil Valois*

Architectural treasures of the National Capital Region: the Canadian Parliament in Ottawa and the Canadian Museum of Civilization in Hull. – T.

Imagine contemplating the magnificent landscape of Parc de la Gatineau, while comfortably seated aboard a steam engine dating back to 1907: **Train à Vapeur Hull-Chelsea-Wakefield** ★ *($26; late May to late Oct, departures Sat to Thu 1:30pm, Fri 10am; 165 Rue Deveault, ☎778-7246, ≈778-5007).* As well as giving you a chance to see beautiful natural sites, this half-day excursion takes you to Wakefield, a charming little English town, where you have two hours to explore and shop. If you're interested in the trip but don't want to take the train both ways, you can cross Gatineau park on bicycle and return by train. Packages including a meal are also available.

 TOUR H : MERRICKVILLE

From Ottawa, take Colonel By Drive South, which runs along the Rideau Canal for some distance. At the end of this road, turn left on Brookfield Road then right on Riverside Drive, which becomes Route 19, and follow it until Kemptville. From here, take Route 43 to Merrickville.

A surprising number of splendid stone buildings line the streets of this small village. Dating back to the 19th century, they bear witness to the former wealth of this hamlet. In 1793, William Mirick undertook the construction of mills next to the waterfalls located at this point on the Rideau River, and this led to the village's prosperity. During the 19th century, development gained pace with the building of the Rideau Canal. The advent of the railways, however, curtailed Merrickville's prosperity, when the town was bypassed by railway builders. One positive repurcussion of this decline, however, is that the village was spared from modernization, and its distinct character seems frozen in time.

Walking alongside the Rideau Canal, the first building you come to is the **Merrickville Public Library** ★ *(Main St.)*, built around the 1890s by William Pearson. This elegant brick building has a gable and a veranda. It was Pearson's daughter Mary who bequeathed this superb dwelling to the town to house its library.

EXPLORING

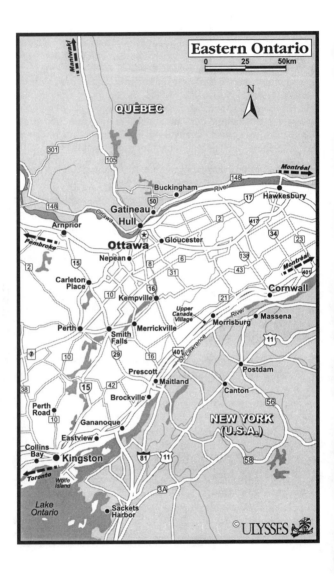

In front, the **Sam Jakes Inn**, now converted to a stylish and comfortable inn, is the former residence of Samuel Jakes, who had it built in 1861.

Continue along Main Street until Saint Lawrence Street.

The **Blockhouse** *($1; mid-May to mid-Oct, every day; ☎692-2581)* is the biggest military building erected along the Rideau Canal to protect the boats using this waterway. It could accommodate up to 50 soldiers, and today houses a small museum.

Turn left on Saint Lawrence Street.

At the edge of the Rideau River is the Merrickville **industrial zone** ★, with the ruins of the mills that once assured the village's prosperity. Among these buildings, the oldest of them built in 1793 by William Mirick, you will see a sawmill, a weaving mill, a flour mill and an oat processing mill. Not far from this area, on Mill Street, is William Mirick's last residence.

Return along Street Lawrence Street.

Saint Lawrence Street is lined with a cluster of shops, each more charming than the last, where you can linger for hours in front of the tempting display windows. For those who wish to explore the other treasures in this delightful village, a small brochure entitled *Merrickville Walking Tour* is also available.

EXPLORING

 TOUR I: UPPER CANADA VILLAGE

Morrisburg would be just another little town if it weren't for the proximity of Upper Canada Village, a remarkable tourist attraction consisting of houses from eight little villages that were flooded when the water level of the river was raised during the construction of the St. Lawrence Seaway. The houses were moved to Crysler Farm Battlefield Park, where they now make up a fascinating historical reproduction of a 19th-century community. The park also has a small monument commemorating the Canadian victory over American troops in the War of 1812.

With 35 buildings, **Upper Canada Village** ★★★ *($9.50; May to Oct, every day 9:30am to 5pm; Crysler Farm Battlefield Park, 11 km east of Morrisburg, on Rte. 2, ☎613-543-3704)* is an outstanding reconstruction of the type of village found in this part of Canada back in the 1860's. The place has a remarkably authentic feel about it, and you will be continually surprised by the extraordinary attention to detail that went into building it. A sawmill, a general store, a farm, a doctor's house... nothing is missing in this village that you can explore on foot or by horse-drawn cart. To top off this almost idyllic tableau, the "villagers" are costumed guides able to answer all your questions. Their carefully designed outfits reflect both their trade and social class. You can spend several hours exploring Upper Canada Village and watching the various inhabitants go about their business (running the sawmill, working on the farm, using the flour mill, etc.).

OUTDOORS

O Since the earliest days of the city, the creation of green spaces was a priority of city leaders, who, over the years, proceeded to lay out vast, beautiful parks and gardens. Whether you are looking for an urban park such as Major's Hill or Rockliffe, or untouched natural spaces like Gatineau Park, Ottawa has a bit of everything to please nature lovers and outdoors people, all of it in or near the city. Hiking, cycling and cross-country skiing are among the sports that are easily practised in the national capital region.

 PARKS

Parc de la Gatineau ★ *(6$; visitor centre is located in Chelsea, also accessible via Boulevard Taché in Hull; ☎827-2020)* is not far from downtown Hull. The 35,000 hectare park was founded during the Depression in 1934 in order to protect the forests from people looking for firewood. It is crossed by a 34 kilometre long road dotted with panoramic lookout points, including as **Belvédère Champlain**, which offer superb views of the lakes, rivers and hills of the region. Outdoor activities can be enjoyed here throughout the year. Hiking and mountain biking trails are open during the summer. There are many lakes in the park, including Lac Meech, which was also the name of onstitutional agreement drawn up nearby but Watersports such as windsurfing, canoeing and also very popular and the park rents small boats s. **Lusk Cave**, formed some 12,500 years ago by from melting glaciers can be explored. During the winter, approximately 190 kilometres of cross-country skiing trails are maintained (*approx. $7 per day*). **Camp Fortune** (*☎827-1717*) has 19 downhill-ski runs, 14 are open at night. It costs $24 during the day and $20 at night.

The **Domaine Mackenzie-King ★★** (*$6 for parking; mid-May to mid-Jun, Wed to Sun 11am to 5pm; mid-Jun to mid-Oct, 11am to 5pm; Rue Barnes in Kingsmere, Parc de la Gatineau, ☎613-239-5000 and 827-2020*). William Lyon Mackenzie King was Prime Minister of Canada from 1921 to 1930, and again from 1935 to 1948. His love of art and horticulture rivalled his interest in politics and he was always happy to get away to his summer residence near Lac Kingsmere, which today is part of Parc de la Gatineau. The estate consists of two houses (one of which is now a charming tea room), a landscaped garden and follies, false ruins that were popular at the time. However, unlike most follies, which were designed to imitate ruins, those on the Mackenzie-King estate are authentic building fragments. For the most part, they were taken from the original Canadian House of Parliament, destroyed by fire in 1916, and from Westminister Palace, damaged by German bombs in 1941.

 OUTDOOR ACTIVITIES

 Hiking

An activity accessible to everyone, hiking outings, from short walks to more challenging excursions in the forest, are possible in various locations in the city and its surroundings. You can stroll along the Rideau Canal or the Ottawa River for a few hours, on pleasant walkways laid out along these waterways; if you enjoy longer excursions, the path along the canal runs all the way to Kingston. Or, you can opt for a nature trek in Gatineau Park.

A beautiful promenade is maintained along the Rideau Canal that is very easy to follow. This path actually constitutes the first metres of the 400-kilometre-long **Rideau Trail**, which runs through the forests and undulating landscapes of Eastern Ontario, along the edge of the Canadian Shield from Ottawa to Kingston. Some parts of the trail are twinned with parallel paths. For a map of the Rideau Trail contact the **Rideau Trail Association**: P.O. Box 14, Kingston, Ont., K7L 4V6.

Parc de la **Gatineau** *(☎827-2020)* offers a great number of hiking trails, over 125 kilometres in all, and just as many chances to discover its beauty. You can explore Lac Pink, a beautiful but polluted lake (you can't swim in it), on a 1.4-kilometres-trail. If you prefer splendid panoramic views, choose Mont-King, a 2.5-kilometre-long trail that leads you to the summit and to gorgeous views of the Ottawa River Valley. And finally, if you have a bit more time and are interested in a fascinating excursion, the Lusk Cave trail is 10.5 kilometres long and leads to 12,500-year-old marble cave.

 Bicycling

The Ottawa region is crisscrossed by no fewer than 150 kilometres of pathways that are very pleasant to meander on foot or by bicycle. Whether you opt for an outing along the Rideau Canal, on the Rockliffe promenade or along the Ottawa River, you will benefit from pleasant landscapes, from peace and quiet and, above all, from trails that are very well laid out for cycling. On Sunday mornings from late May to early September, cyclists are in seventh heaven as these routes are closed to automobile traffic. Maps of Ottawa's bicycle and walking paths are available at the capital Infocentre.

Bicycle Rental

Cyco's: 5 Hawthorne Ave., ☎567-8180.
Dow's Lake Pavilion: ☎232-1001.

OUTDOORS

Cruises

As soon as the fine weather arrives, cruises are operated along the waterways surrounding Ottawa. You can take part, seeing the city from a different angle and drifting quietly on the waves. Several companies offer such excursions, notably:

Ottawa Riverboat
30 Murray St., Ottawa, Ontario, K1N 5M4, ☎562-4888.

 Skating

Imagine lacing on a pair of skates and gliding uninterrupted over 8 kilometres of ice. Every winter, as soon as the **Rideau Canal** has frozen over, in late December or early January, the canal is transformed into a vast skating rink, one of the longest in the world. The ice surface is cleared and maintained for the pleasure of skaters of all ages. A heated cabin is at the disposal of visitors just a few steps from the National Arts Centre to allow skaters to lace up away from the cold.

Dow's Lake also possesses a heated lodge in which sports can don their skates, warm up and have a bite to eat.

Ice Conditions: ☎239-5234.

 Cross-Country Skiing

In winter, when there's a thick layer of snow, **Parc de la Gatineau** maintains no less than 200 kilometres of cross-country ski trails. These trails, 47 in all, are sure to delight skiers of all levels.

ACCOMMODATIONS

A wide choice of types of accommodation to fit every budget is available in Ottawa. Most places are very comfortable and offer a number of extra services. Prices vary according to the type of accommodation and the quality-to-price ratio is generally good, but remember to add the 7% G.S.T (federal Goods and Services Tax) and the provincial sales tax of 5%. The Goods and Services Tax is refundable for non-residents in certain cases (see p 51). A credit card will make reserving a room much easier, since in many cases payment for the first night is required.

Many hotels and inns offer considerable discounts to employees of corporations or members of automobile clubs (CAA, AAA). Be sure to ask about corporate and other discounts as they are often very easy to obtain. You'll also find many coupons in the brochures given out for free by the Travel Associations. Often, if the hotel is not booked, special arrangements can be made for you for no extra charge. For example, you can ask for a room with a better view or a corner room for the same price as a standard one.

The symbols found in parentheses following the name of the establishment will help you make your choice. Take note, however, that these may not apply to each room in a place. You will find the list of symbols and their explanations at the beginning of the book. Since most of the accommodations offer a private bathroom with each room, we have only mentioned those with shared bathrooms.

Hotels

Hotels rooms abound, and range from modest to luxurious. Most hotel rooms come equipped with a private bathroom. There are several internationally reputed hotels in Ontario, including several beauties in the Canadian Pacific chain.

Inns

Often set up in beautiful historic houses, inns offer quality lodging. There are a lot of these establishments which are more charming and usually more picturesque than hotels. Many are furnished with beautiful period pieces. Breakfast is often included.

 UPPER TOWN

Right in the city, on the Lebreton flats, travellers will find a small, friendly **campground** *(free for children under 12; June to early Sep; tents only; ☎236-1251)* easily reached by a bicycle path as well as by car or bus. It is run by the National Capital Commission and has 200 places. Toilets, showers and picnic tables. Reservations are not accepted.

Visitors can stay in proximity of the Parliament Buildings on Albert Street, which changes in this part of Ottawa – the shops and the hubbub of downtown giving way to a quiet residential district (some may even fault it for being virtually devoid of shops). This area boasts two charming inns. The first of these, the **Doral Inn** *($69; K; 468 Albert St., K1R 5B5, ☎230-8055)* is set up in a lovely Victorian house and contains about forty rooms. Just off the hall are two small lounges appointed with secondhand furniture, giving them an antiquated look that will appeal to some. The rooms are simply furnished and offer decent comfort for the price. All are equipped with private

```
Ulysses's Favorites

For history lovers:
       Château Laurier (p 113).

For Victorian charm:
       King Edward (p 112), Olde Bytown B&B (p 111) and
       Carmichael Inn (p 110).

For elegant decor:
       Paterson B&B (p 112).

For businesspeople:
       Westin (p 113) and Sheraton (p 110).
```

bathrooms and some also have kitchenettes. Rooms can be rented for the day, the week, or the month.

Next door, the **Albert House** *($80 bkfst incl.; 478 Albert St., K1R 5B5, ☎236-4479)* is also located in an appealing residence. There are only 17 rooms, giving it a pleasant family atmosphere. Each of the rooms is perfectly maintained and decorated with care.

At the western end of Queen Street stands the **Travelodge** *($85; ⊛, ⊘, K; 402 Queen St., K1R 5A7, ☎236-1133 or 1-800-578-7878, ⇔236-2317)*. An attractive red-brick building whose modern architecture manifests a certain studied elegance, it gives a misleading idea of the rooms within. Though relatively spacious, their decor is somewhat lacking in charm. Moreover, guests are constantly assailed by a succession of garish advertisements placed all over the hotel (elevator, reception), to remind guests of the hotel's affiliations, but ultimately attesting to its want of class. Fortunately, many little advantages, such as a coffee machines, hair dryers and fax reception at no extra charge, make these minor inconveniences negligible. Some of the rooms have kitchenettes.

The **Rideau View Inn** *($70 sb, $85 pb; 177 Frank St., K2P 0X4, ☎236-9309 or 1-800-658-3564, ⇔ 237-6842)* is set in a large Edwardian house furnished in period style. Facing a small public park with tennis courts, this non-smoking residence offers seven rooms, two of them with private bath and one with a sitting room. Guests can also use the lounge with its fireplace and television. A terrace on the top floor is also available to guests.

Victoria Park Suites *($85; △, K, ☺; 377 O'Connor St., K2P 2M2, ☎567-7275, ≈567-1161)* is a good spot to keep in mind if you want to be just a few steps from Parliament Hill with your own kitchenette and an impeccably kept room.

In the vicinity of Parliament Hill, the stark and old-fashioned building of the **Capital Hill** hotel *($90; ℜ; 88 Albert St., K1P 5E9, ☎235-1413 or 1-800-463-7705, ≈235-6047)* harbours well-kept, relatively large and comfortable rooms with rather commonplace decors, making it a passable choice for nights when other hotels in the city are full.

The **Lord Elgin Hotel** *($90; ℜ, ♿; 100 Elgin St., K1P 5K8, ☎235-3333 or 1-800-267-4298, ≈235-3223)* is among those untimely Ottawan institutions. Very few pieces of furniture, however, have managed to conserve any traces of its past, save for the lobby, which still has a pretty centre light and an antique mobile hanging from the ceiling. The rooms, for their part, are large and decorated with modern furnishings that may fail to lend the charm of yesteryear but make for a pleasant stay nonetheless.

The economy hotel chain Days Inn has taken over a charming little hotel that occupies a 19th-century building: the **Hotel Roxborough** *($95 bkfst incl.; ℜ; 123 Metcalfe St., K1P 5L9, ☎237-9300 or 1-800-329-7466, ≈237-2163)*. This spot is calm, and rooms offer two double beds or a queen-size bed. The hotel also has a restaurant that serves breakfast. The location is ideal, near Elgin Street and the National Arts Centre.

As you enter the **Delta** *($99; ≈, ℜ, △, ☺; 361 Queen St., K1R 7S9, ☎238-6000, ≈238-2290)* you will straightaway notice the efforts made to create a more intimate atmosphere than at the standard downtown chain hotel. The glass ceiling allows plenty of light to penetrate the vast lobby. It also boasts ficuses, mahogany chairs and a warm fireplace to cosy up to during the winter. The rooms are of a good size and are furnished with comfortable mahogany pieces. Finally, children will be thrilled with the pool's long waterslide.

If there is one hotel that has neglected to keep up with the times, it is certainly the **Citadel** *($109; 101 Lyon St., K1R 5T9, ☎237-3600 or 1-800-567-3600, ≈237-2351)*. Indeed, it seems that few efforts have been made to win visitors over: the hall is adorned with a few stunted plastic plants and the imitation marble walls do not succeed in giving the place any soul. Moreover, as if to match the environment, even the welcome is dour. The hotel does have comfortable rooms, however, and offers several excursion packages.

The **Radisson** *($125; ≈, △, ⊛, ℛ, ⅙; 100 Kent St., K1P 5R7, ☎238-1122 or 1-800-333-3333, ≈783-4229)* differs greatly from its neighbour, the Citadel. Though this concrete high-rise may seem common and somewhat short on charm at first glance, several little details have been seen to in order to offer the quality of lodging provided by other big hotels in the city, which translates into a polite welcome and a foyer sufficiently elegant to be inviting. An effort has also been made where the rooms are concerned, which, though decorated with beige formica furniture, are eminently comfortable. Finally, the fitness centre is very pleasant.

At first glance, the **Albert at Bay** *($110; K, ⊘; 435 Albert St., K1R 7X4, ☎238-8858 or 1-800-267-6644, ≈238-1433)*, a banal building, looks more like a high-rise apartment complex that has seen better days than a hotel. This place, however, is a good choice for practical reasons rather than charm. Every suite boasts a bedroom, a living room, a dining area and a fully equipped kitchenette (microwave oven, coffee-maker). Also, over and above the comfort of a real apartment, guests benefit from the perks of a hotel, such as a daily cleaning service and a fitness centre.

In the heart of downtown stands the high-rise building housing the **Minto** hotel *($115; K, ⅙, ℛ; 433 Laurier Ave. W., ☎232-2200 or 1-800-267-3377, ≈232-6962, www.minto.com/corp.html)*. The rooms here are not decorated with any particular originality, but they are perfectly suited to business travellers, each one of them having a desk large enough to work at comfortably, as well as a small living room and a kitchenette. In the basement, visitors will find a shopping mall and restaurants.

Some prefer older establishments filled with antiques and an elegant decor, still others opt for modern styling and the utmost in service. Those who fit into the latter category will appreciate the very modern **Sheraton** *($119; ≈, ℜ, △, ⊘, &;150 Albert St., K1P 5G2, ☎238-1500 or 1-800-489-8333, ≈235-2723)*, with its conference halls, large rooms with offices, telephones with voice-mail, hair dryers and fitness centre with pool, sauna and whirlpool.

With over 200 rooms comprising a kitchenette, small living room and balcony, the **Cartier Place & Towers** *($120; ≈, △, ⊘, K; 180 Cooper St., ☎236-5000 or 1-800-236-8399, ≈238-3842)* is a choice place for those wishing to spend a few days in the capital. The establishment also boasts a fitness centre and a pleasant patio surrounded by a bit of greenery.

 Set in an imposing old house, the **Carmichael Inn & Spa** *($125 bkfst incl.; ℜ; 46 Cartier St., K2P 1J3, ☎236-4667, ≈563-7529)* is part of Ottawa's heritage. This non-smoking establishment has 11 rooms, decorated with antiques and fitted with queen-size beds.

🛏 LOWER TOWN AND SANDY HILL

Those seeking low-priced accommodations during the summer can rent one of the basic but adequate rooms in the residence halls at both **Ottawa University** *(85 University St., ☎562-5771, ≈562-5157)* and **Carleton University** *(1125 Colonel By Promenade, ☎520-5611, ≈520-3952)*.

Right next to the Rideau Centre, in the middle of everything, you will see an imposing building that once housed the city's prison. Entirely remodeled, it now houses a **youth hostel** *($18,95 per person, $37 for a room; K; 75 Nicholas St., K1N 7B9, ☎235-2595)*. In addition to dormitories and three rooms, the hostel has a fully-equipped communal kitchen.

Those with an appreciation for old buildings will also be delighted with the **Lampman House** bed & breakfast *($65 bkfst* *incl.; sb; 369 Daly Ave., K1N 6G8, ☎241-3696, ⌨789-8360)*, a lovely Georgian-style residence. This row house, a testament to the early days of this Ottawa district, boasts three rooms elegantly decorated with antique furnishings and curios.

The Sandy Hill district is sure to charm fans of the Victorian style. If you count yourselves among them but do not have the means for extravagances, the **McGee Inn** *($68 bkfst incl. and sb, $78 bkfst incl. and pb; ⊛, ≡; 185 Daly Ave., K1N 6E8, ☎237-6089)* is a good choice. This red-brick house, erected in 1886 has succeeded in retaining its original cachet. Admittedly, the rooms are simply decorated, but they are tasteful nonetheless. Moreover, the place is well-kept and all the rooms are air conditioned.

Dating from the early 20th century but entirely renovated, **L'Auberge du Marché** *($69 bkfst incl.; 87 Guigues St., K1N 5H8, ☎241-6610 or 1-800-465-0079)* is a little house that reflects the charm of its proprietor. There are three rooms upstairs and a shared bathroom, as well as a suite on the ground floor with a private bathroom, a full kitchen, and a small lounge with sofa-bed and cable television. Breakfast varies each day, but is always plentiful and refined. Guests have a private entrance allowing them to come and go as they please.

The **Auberge Wildflower** *($69 sb, $85 pb; 376 Wilbrod St., ☎565-1887 or 1-800-278-4966, ⌨565-7751)* is another good place in the area for those seeking economical accommodations. Though lacking the character of turn-of-the-century residences, this lovely house has the advantage of offering modern comforts.

Located in a quiet neighbourhood and affording a superb view of Strathcona Park, the **Olde Bytown Bed and Breakfast** *($75 bkfst incl.; pb, sb; 459 Laurier Ave. E., K1N 6R4, ☎565-7939, ⌨565-7981)* is a choice place for those who appreciate the cachet of turn-of-the-century Victorian houses. The B & B's every room is meticulously kept and graced with beautiful antiques, flowered wallpaper and old artifacts. There are seven wonderfully cosy rooms in which guests could easily spend hours daydreaming.

The impeccably kept **Gasthaus Switzerland** *($78; 89 Daly Ave., K1N 6E6, ☎237-0335, ⇒594-3327)* is a small, unpretentious hotel whose Swiss-chalet-style decor may be a little too colourful for some tastes. You will have a restful stay, however, for the owners are friendly, breakfasts are plentiful, and the atmosphere is pleasant.

The **Auberge King Edward** *($80; 525 King Edward Ave., K1N 7N3, ☎565-6700)* is set up in a very beautiful house dating from the beginning of the century and, in keeping with the period of the building, all the rooms are graced with antiques and myriad old curios. This somewhat cluttered decor has undeniable charm and imparts an atmosphere of calm and well-being to the establishment. The inn boasts two charming living rooms, as well as three exceedingly well-kept bedrooms (one with a private bathroom).

If you prefer the comfort of a suite at a reasonable price, **Les Suites** *($90; ≈, ℜ, △, ⊛, ⚕, ✘; 130 Besserer St., Ottawa K1N 9M9, ☎232-2000, ⇒232-1242)* welcomes you. Just a few steps from the Rideau Centre, you will enjoy a one- or two-bedroom apartment with full kitchen, dining room and lounge. Children under 18 stay free. The hotel also has an indoor pool.

With its dark blue foyer trimmed with steel and wood, the **Novotel** *($99; ℜ, ≈, △, ⊘; 33 Nicholas St., K1N 9M7, ☎230-3033 or 1-800-NOVOTEL, ⇒230-7865)* stands apart from the city's Victorian hotels. This modernity is not without refinement, despite the fact that some will describe it as cold. The rooms are somewhat warmer, however, their dark colours pleasantly adorning the spacious quarters, all boasting a rather large bathroom.

At the very end of Wilbrod Street stands the magnificent stone building housing the **Paterson B&B** *($135 bkfst incl.; 500 Wilbrod St., K1N 6N2, ☎565-8996, ⇒565- 6546)*, one of the district's gems. This monumental Queen Anne house was entirely renovated in 1992 by experts who saw to it that its treasures of yesteryear were preserved. Its cut-stone façade proudly heralds the splendours awaiting inside. As such, the first room guests enter displays panelled walls and ceilings, finely-wrought wainscotting, beautiful antique furniture, carpets and a grand wooden staircase leading to the rooms upstairs.

The Victorian decor of the four rooms combines antique furnishings, floral prints, and frames and curios of all kinds. The establishment's good taste extends to the private bathrooms, all exceedingly charming and impeccably clean. Some rooms benefit from small boudoirs, where guests can watch TV. Breakfast is served in a vast and elegant dining room. A very gracious welcome completes this idyllic scene.

The **Westin Hotel** *($135; ≈, ℛ, ⌂, ⊛, ⊘, &, ✗; 11 Colonel By Dr., ☎560-7000, ⊷569-2013)* has what may be the most enviable location in Ottawa, facing the Rideau Canal, opposite the National Arts Centre and right in the heart of Ottawa's bustle. It is part of the complex that includes the Rideau Centre shopping mall and the Ottawa Convention Centre. Rooms are very spacious and extremely comfortable, offering magnificent views of the canal. The hotel has a very good restaurant, Daly's (excellent atmosphere, interesting and refined cuisine), and even a happening night club. Very good weekend packages are usually available.

The opulence and luxury of the **Château Laurier** *($150; ≈; ⌂; &; 1 Rideau St., Ottawa K1N 8S7, ☎241-1414 or 1-800-441-1414, ⊷562-7030)* (see p 78), part of the Canadian Pacific hotel chain, will appeal to those who like to rave about beautiful things. Upon entering the hotel, visitors will be swept away by the decor: wainscotted walls, cornices, bas reliefs and antiques. The lobby itself gives an idea of the comfort and elegance of the rooms, all stocked with wooden furnishings, plush couches and comfortable beds. Undeniably pleasant, the rooms combine onetime elegance with today's comforts. Two very good restaurants and a sports centre with a lovely Art-Deco swimming pool add to the place's overall effect (see p 127).

THE GLEBE

Located on a quiet street in the pleasant Glebe district, the **Blue Spruces Bed & Breakfast** *($85 bkfst incl.; 187 Glebe Ave., K1S 2C6, ☎236-8521, ⊷231-3730)* is enchanting. This elegant Edwardian house welcomes only non-smokers and is furnished with 19th-century Victorian and Canadian antiques. The luxury of the decor is rivalled only by that of the bedding. And if that is not enough, the breakfasts and the hospitality of the owner will round out the enchantment.

 OUTSIDE OTTAWA

Those who must stay in the Ottawa region but do not wish to enter the city itself can find accommodations along Highway 417, where three establishments succeed each other: the **Comfort Inn** *($82; 1252 Michael St., K1J 7T1, ☎744-2900 or 1-800-424-6423, ⇝746-0836)*, the **Chimo** *($115; ⊘, ≈, ℛ; 1199 Joseph Cyr St., ☎744-1060 or 1-800-387-9779, ⇝744-7845)*, which rivals the other hotels in the city by providing modern sports facilities, and the **Welcome Inn** *($85; 1220 Michael St., ☎748-7800 or 1-800-387-4381, ⇝748-0499)*.

 HULL

The **Auberge de la Gare** *($74 bkfst incl.; 205 Boulevard St-Joseph, J8Y 3X3, ☎778-8085 or 773-4273, ⇝595-2021)* is a simple, conventional hotel that offers good value for your money. The service is both courteous and friendly, and the rooms are clean and well kept, albeit nondescript.

The small, austere lobby of the **Hôtel Best Western** *($79; ≈, ℛ; 131 Rue Laurier, J8X 3W3, ☎770-8550 or 1-800-265-8550)* is hardly inviting. The rooms, decorated with modern furniture, are neither cozy nor luxurious but nonetheless comfortable.

The **Hôtel Ramada Plaza** *($95; ℛ, ≈, ♿; 35 Rue Laurier, J9Y 4E9, ☎778-6111 or 1-800-567-9607, ⇝778-8548)* is located opposite the Musée des Civilisations. It is a simple-looking building in the typical chain-hotel style, and the rooms are stocked with nondescript, functional furnishings. During the low season, you can take advantage of the hotel's economical package rates.

MERRICKVILLE

The **Sam Jakes Inn** *($181 ½b; ℛ, ⊛; 118 Main St. E., K0G 1N0, ☎269-3711 or 1-800-567-4667, ⊷269-3713)* occupies a splendid and very elegant early 19th-century residence. Rooms are comfortable and decorated with fine old furniture. Excellent meals are available in the big dining rooms on the ground floor. The courteous hospitality and the quiet atmosphere make this inn a choice spot for a restful stay.

RESTAURANTS

The city of Ottawa abounds in restaurants of all kinds. Whether you are partial to steak or roast beef, fish or French, Italian, Asian or other specialties, the city's restaurants are sure to fulfil your expectations. A number of them are open for both lunch and dinner; keep in mind, however, that satisfying your hunger after 11pm can prove difficult.

These restaurants generally offer a good selection of dishes and sometimes a fixed-price menu consisting of an appetizer, a main course and coffee. Whatever your choice, be advised that in the great majority of cases, prices do not include taxes. You must add 7% federal tax (GST) and 8% provincial tax (PST) to your bill, as well as a 15% tip (or more, according to the quality of the service).

Unless otherwise indicated, the prices mentioned in the guide are for a meal for one person, not including taxes, drinks and tip.

$	$10 or less
$$	$10 to $20
$$$	$20 to $30
$$$$	$30 or more

RESTAURANTS BY TYPE OF CUISINE

Pubs
   D'Arcy McGee (p 121)
   Earl of Sussex (p 125)

Québécoise cuisine
   La Soupière (p 131)

Steaks
   Al's Steak and Seafood
   (p 123)
   Connaught (p 122)
   Friday's (p 122)
   Tucker's Marketplace
   (p 127)
   Sam Jakes Inn (p 133)

Tex-Mex
   Blue Cactus (p 125)

Variety
   Marché Mövenpick
   (p 123)
   Santé (p 124)

Vietnamese
   Good Morning Vietnam
   (p 123)

Ulysses' Favorites

Ottawa and Hull institutions:
      Le Métro (p 123), Café Henry Burger (p 132) and
      Domus (p 128).

For innovative cuisine:
      Echo Wine Café (p 120).

For desserts:
      Memories (p 125).

For elegant decor:
      Wilfrid's (p 127) and Friday's (p 122).

For the terrasse:
      National Arts Centre Café (p 120) and
      Le Twist (p 131).

This chapter offers you a selection of a few good restaurants
in the city. If you would like more information on Ottawa's
restaurants, consult the www.dine.net web site.

THE RIDEAU CANAL

The menu at the **Ritz on the Canal** *($$; 375 Queen Elizabeth Dr., at Fifth Ave., ☎238-8998)* differs somewhat from those of its sister establishments (see p 122, 127) in that it also features "gourmet" pizzas baked in a wood-burning oven. This restaurant is particularly appreciated in summer, on account of its outstanding setting and huge terrace facing a part of the canal that resembles a bay. No smoking.

 Those eager for new culinary experiences will be delighted with the **Echo Wine Café** *($$-$$$; 221 Echo Dr., ☎234-1528)*. Day after day, the chef creates unique dishes blending unusual flavours, such as fillet of salmon with spicy *papadum* on a bed of curried rice enhanced with sweet apple sauce. Diners may hesitate to sample such a combination but will be delighted with the result. To better accompany each of the dishes, a selection of wines sold by the glass is available. The dishes are all delectable, but saving a little room for dessert is essential as these are equally innovative and mouthwatering.

The **Café of the National Arts Centre** *($$$; 53 Elgin St., ☎594-5127)* offers an unbeatable view of the teeming activity on the Rideau Canal, with boats in the summer and skaters in the winter. During the summer months, meals are served on a comfortable, well-designed terrace. Beyond a doubt, this is one of the most pleasant outdoor terraces in town. Refined Canadian cooking is offered; the chef makes inventive use of quality products from various regions of Canada. Grilled Atlantic salmon is a specialty. Not to be missed are the wonderful desserts. Prices are on the high side, however, unless a fixed-price menu is offered, which is unfortunately rare.

UPPER TOWN

If you love true American-style pizza with plenty of toppings, try **The Colonnade** *($-$$; 280 Metcalfe St., ☎237-3179)* which has had the market cornered for a while now. This spot is very simple and is divided into two parts, one of them supposedly more chic than the other. The centrepiece, however, is the pizza. It comes with cheese; choosing the rest is up to you.

If you are looking for a good but simple Mexican meal, the friendly **Pancho Villa** *($-$$; 361 Elgin St., ☎234-8872)* can provide it. Just next door is **Lois and Frimas**, whose excellent home-made ice creams keep people coming back again and again.

If there is one place in Ottawa in which to enjoy a good meal in an unparalleled ambiance, it is definitely the **D'Arcy McGee** *($$; 44 Sparks St., ☎230-4433)*. This typical Irish pub, located a stone's throw from Parliament Hill, is the haunt par excellence of the political staff. Perfectly warm and frequented by a clientele of all ages, it has become one of the city's absolute musts.

The Radisson hotel has two restaurants. The first, **Café Toulouse** *($$; 100 Kent St., ☎238-1122)*, is set up on the ground floor in a vast, comfortable room adorned with plants, wainscotting and large picture windows looking out on the street. The fare here is simple and humble (burgers, salads, steaks), but the place's main advantage is being one of the few pleasant restaurants in the area, which is particularly deserted on weekends. **La Rotonde** *($$)* is on the top floor. Here you can enjoy your meal while taking in panoramic views (this is a revolving restaurant) of the city.

A little further west, the **Fairouz** restaurant *($$; 343 Somerset St. West, ☎233-1536)* occupies another of these fine, renovated Victorian houses. If you like Lebanese specialties, go no further: the food here will delight you.

In terms of decor, **Johnny Farina** *($$; 216 Elgin St., ☎565-5155)* has no cause to be envious of other very trendy restaurants on Elgin Street. Its vast dining room, graced with very high coffered ceilings, is adorned with a ceramic-tile floor, brick walls and a lovely black staircase. It is ideal for dining with friends, as you can have a good time and eat well without spending a fortune. The menu features dishes prepared with a modicum of originality, such as tortellini with goat cheese sauce and pizzas baked in a wood-burning oven. Moreover, while waiting for your meal, you can watch the cooks in action, for the open kitchen looks directly onto the dining room. The

RESTAURANTS

only thing to find fault with here is the TV, always on (though at low volume) in the corner.

🦐 Elgin Street is home to an institution known to just about everyone in town, the **Ritz** *($$; 274 Elgin St., ☎235-7027)*. Waiting is almost obligatory at this Italian restaurant, which does not accept reservations. Its pasta dishes are deservedly renowned. Fortunately, this restaurant now has younger siblings. The **Ritz Uptown** *(226 Nepean, ☎238-8752)* is set in an old house, and reservations are accepted.

Not far from the Ritz Uptown, in another pretty little house, is **Fiori's** *($$$; 239 Nepean St., ☎232-1377)*, an Italian restaurant with excellent food. The veal dishes are especially delectable. The restaurant is small, friendly and full of charm. Service is warm and attentive. This comes at a price, of course, but it is worth it.

At the very end of the lobby of the Lord Elgin hotel, the **Connaught** *($$-$$$; 100 Elgin St., ☎235-3333)* is bathed in sunlight pouring in through its large glass veranda. The restaurant opens at the crack of dawn, when you can enjoy a good breakfast. The dinner menu features various dishes, including filet mignon and prime ribs.

A little to the east, toward Elgin Street, **Chez Jean-Pierre** *($$$; 210 Somerset St. West, ☎235-9711)* does not have the most inviting of façades, and the interior decor is not its strong point, but these are things you can live with, for the fine French cuisine and the service are solid. This is a restaurant where quality is a long-time tradition.

A feeling of well-being will sweep over you as soon as you walk into **Friday's** *($$$; 150 Elgin St., ☎237-5353)*, which occupies a magnificent Victorian house built in 1875. With its large antique-decorated rooms, its big wooden tables and its high-backed chairs, which exude old-fashioned charm, the place is irresistible. Its rooms have been transformed into dining rooms where a relaxing atmosphere prevails. If the decor doesn't win you over, the succulent roast surely will. Of course, with all this going for it, Friday's has a devout following, so reservations are recommended.

🏛 **Le Métro** *($$$; 315 Somerset St. West, ☎230-8123)* is undoubtedly one of the best eating spots in town. The *escargots* with roquefort in pastry are a true joy, as are the steak tartare or simple beef fillet with *béarnaise* sauce. The opulent, harmonious decor, the quiet atmosphere and the big, comfortable leather chairs assure you a relaxing and delicious evening.

Elgin Street boasts another choice place for real beef lovers: **Al's Steak and Seafood House** *($$$-$$$$; 327 Elgin St., ☎828-8349)*. This stylish restaurant has been delighting palates with perfectly tender and juicy prime beef for over 20 years now. Moreover, though the place's reputation was built on its toothsome steak, its seafood never disappoints.

LOWER TOWN

Rideau Street

Having a good meal in a shopping centre may seem illusory... And yet, **MarcheLino Mövenpick** *($; Rideau St., at Sussex Dr.)*, in the Rideau Centre, attracts crowds of happy diners. The restaurant's recipe for success is simple: a large dining-room, attractively decorated with plants and wooden tables, and delicious, quickly-prepared dishes from fresh, quality ingredients. In this lively place, everyone is free to stroll about, choosing their dishes from one of the various stations where sushi, salads, pasta, quiches and all sorts of other dishes sure to please the most demanding palates are prepared before your eyes.

Heading east from the Rideau Centre, you will reach the Bytowne repertory cinema and its neighbour, **Good Morning Vietnam** *($-$$; 323 Rideau St., ☎789-4080)*. This little restaurant with its very plain decor lets the food do the talking, especially the hot and sour soup and the spring rolls.

The delicacies of Louisiana cooking are yours to discover at the **Cajun Attic** *($$; 594 Rideau St., ☎789-1185)*, where each dish is more succulent than the last. You'll choose from favourites

RESTAURANTS

like chicken jambalaya or cajun curry with pecans. According to many this is the best cajun food in the city if not the region!

Hidden right at the end of the street, a little before crossing the Rideau River, is **Mukut** *($$; 610 Rideau St., ☎789-2220)*, a very good Indian restaurant. Only the New Delhi on Bank Street can match the exquisite quality of the dishes prepared here. Located in an uninviting mini-mall, it lacks charm, but the food is wonderful.

🦫 Located on the second floor of a building facing the Rideau Centre, **Santé** *($$$; 45 Rideau St., ☎241-7113)* is easy to miss, so keep your eyes peeled; its Californian, Thai and Caribbean specialties are true delights, especially the Bangkok noodles. This spot is an oasis of quiet repose with big bay windows opening onto some of the city's main attractions. Save room for something from the tempting dessert list. Attentive service.

Around Byward Market

Although the surroundings of the Byward Market form the area most visited by tourists and locals alike, there are disappointingly few worthwhile restaurants. On the other hand, if you have sudden pangs of hunger or thirst, this is the place to be, especially in the summer. There are a number of friendly outdoor cafés and plenty of pedestrian traffic. In short, it is lively and very pleasant.

Sweet teeth will want to sample **Beaver Tails** *(at George St. and William St.)*. Do not be alarmed, these are merely delicious treats made from sugared deep-fried dough, something of a cross between a doughnut and a biscuit.

Those craving a bite to eat after visiting one of the museums on Sussex Drive should stop by **Café Quo Vadis** *($; Sussex Dr. at Clarence St.)*, set up in a large, rather cold space decorated with art work (which you can purchase). You will undoubtedly find something with which to appease your hunger here, for the place serves a good selection of cakes and coffees.

Rickety tables, mismatched chairs and all kinds of old-fashioned knick-knacks make up the somewhat ill-assorted but oddly charming decor at **Café Wim** *($; 537 Sussex Dr.)*. Early in the morning, you can enjoy a good breakfast here (pancakes, eggs, sausages and fresh fruit salad). The place is also pleasant at lunch time, the sun pouring in through the large picture windows and the menu featuring simple dishes, including salads and sandwiches.

The **Earl of Sussex** *($; 431 Sussex Dr., ☎562-5544)* is a quintessential English pub: relaxed ambiance, woodwork, simple and nourishing fare and, above all, a wonderful selection of domestic and imported beers on tap. The place is fairly hopping from noon to late afternoon.

🎂 **Memories** *($; 7 Clarence St., ☎232-1882)* is almost always packed. Why? Because almost everyone in Ottawa comes to try the many desserts that have made its reputation. The selection of cakes and pies of all sorts is so impressive that it can be hard to choose. But the greatest temptation may fall on the delicious, oversized portions of apple pie. Light meals (interesting soups, sandwiches, salads) are also available. The coffee is good.

For a *gelato* without equal, **Piccolo Grande** *($; at the corner of Murray and Parent streets)* is the place to go. The queues bear witness to this. You will find a big assortment of Italian ices of exceptional quality as well as Neuhaus Belgian chocolates.

A delightful little café looking out on Byward Market, **Planet Coffee** *($; George St.)* offers a good selection of coffees and pastries.

Some spots draw attention more for their decor than for their food. This is the case of **Zak's Diner** *($; 89 Clarence St., ☎238-7182)*, whose bright lights and Coca-Cola signs are meant to make it look like a 1950s American diner. The menu seems not to have evolved since that time, with the usual hamburgers, milk shakes and fries, served in large portions. This is a pleasant spot for breakfast.

Blue Cactus *($-$$; 2 Byward Market, ☎241-7061)* is a Tex-Mex restaurant with the usual megacocktails, *nachos* (try the very filling Blue Cactus *nachos*), *fajitas* and so on. The atmosphere at this spot, which is popular with young people, may be a little too lively for some.

For years now, **Clair de lune** *($-$$; 81B Clarence St.)* has been delighting diners, who appreciate its laid-back ambiance as well as its menu, which features good, simple dishes.

What will undoubtedly catch your eye at the **Mangia** restaurant *($-$$; 121 Clarence St., ☎562-4725)* are the large picture windows, for the menu offers no surprises: pasta and good pizzas. The fact remains that the place is ideal for having a bite to eat on a sunny day, and this without spending a fortune.

If, by any chance, you are looking for something a little different, head to the **Silk Road Café** *($-$$; 47 William St., ☎241-4254)*, which serves Afghan food. Though very simple, this little restaurant, whose decor essentially consists of salmon-pink and black walls as well as a few works of art for sale, has a certain cachet. The lunch menu features less exotic dishes, such as quiches, chicken salads and burgers.

For reasonably priced Indian food, you might consider **Sharfarli** *($-$$; Dalhousie St. at Clarence St.)*, a small, modest-looking restaurant where you will enjoy no less than excellent tandoori dishes and perfectly fresh nan bread.

If getting better acquainted with the flavours of Morrocco appeals to you, head to the **Casablanca** *($$; 41 Clarence St., ☎789-7855)*, the restaurant, whose tasty dishes offer a wonderful opportunity to discover unique flavours and aromas.

The **Café Crêpe de France** *($$; 76 Murray St., ☎241-1220)* is worth a visit for its Breton-style crepes, its salads or for its weekend brunch. The setting is congenial, with exposed brick, red-and-white-checked tablecloths, and subdued lighting. Big bay windows let in plenty of daylight. In the summer, you can opt for the pretty little outdoor terrace. Besides crepes, different full-course meals are offered each day, but they aren't as good. This is an ideal spot for a light lunch or for a dessert crepe in the evening.

Set in a small, delightful space, where you will feel at ease almost immediately, the **Mama Grazzy** restaurant *($$; 25 George St., ☎241-8656)* also boasts original, delicious and delightful Italian cooking.

If you don't feel like trying anything new, have been craving some family-style cooking and just want a good menu with ordinary dishes, consider **Tucker's Marketplace** *($$; 61 York Street, ☎241-6525)*. Among the choices is the all-you-can-eat roast beef.

Those who are particularly fond of the cuisine at the **Ritz** restaurant *($$; 89 Clarence St., ☎789-9797)* will be pleased to know that the city boasts a second one near Byward Market.

Vittoria Trattoria *($$; 35 William St.)* boasts a pretty dining room: its stone walls and large windows opening out on the street give it an unparalleled cachet. There is also a second large dining room, likewise graced with a stone wall, upstairs; unfortunately, its ambiance is not as warm. Patrons will enjoy good Italian fare here.

Would a jaunt to the Château Laurier strike your fancy? If you go in for this kind of treat but do not wish to squander a fortune on a single meal, head to **Wilfrid's** *($$; 1 Rideau St., ☎241-1414)* come lunch time. You will thus be regaled with a warm dining room, comfortable armchairs, an unobstructed view of the Rideau Canal and a delicious but affordable lunch (prices of *à-la-carte* dishes are around $10). The dinner menu is more refined and more expensive *($$$-$$$$)*. Coming here for breakfast can also be very pleasant, but will cost you at least $10. On Sundays, however, it is best to opt for **Zoe's**, for a delicious brunch *($22.95)* served in a quiet and elegant ambiance.

Another institution in Ottawa is **The Fish Market** restaurant *($$-$$$; 54 York St., ☎241-3474)*, set up on the approaches to the Byward Market and known throughout the capital since 1979. The dining-room is decorated with nets, buoys and other objects related to fishing, as is only right and proper in an establishment specializing in fish, shellfish and seafood, always impeccably fresh. Two other rooms on the first floor meet other needs. **Coasters**, whose large picture windows look out on the bustling market, is just as pleasant. Dishes here are less sophisticated (fish n' chips) and more moderately priced, but quite good. The third room, **Vineyards**, is the place to go if all you want is a drink (good selection of wine by the glass) and a bite to eat. Shows are sometimes featured here.

 Domus Café *($$$; 85 Murray St., ☎241-6007)* is undoubtedly one of the best restaurants in Ottawa. The food is refined and innovative, made with the freshest of ingredients; its success is derived from original combinations of international flavours. Recipes are drawn from the many cookbooks sold at the adjacent store. The menu changes every day, but some of the most popular items keep reappearing. The choice is never exhaustive, but the selection is interesting enough to make it difficult to decide. The desserts, limited to a choice of four or five, are of a calibre unequalled in Ottawa. The wine list includes excellent Californian wines, some of them available by the glass. And finally, try the Sunday brunch. It is divine and well worth the wait (reservations are not accepted for brunch).

OTTAWA'S NEIGHBOURHOODS

Heading west along Somerset Street West, you first cross **Chinatown,** between Bronson and Booth streets, which does not have any outstanding restaurants, though the more popular ones always seem to be filled to capacity. **Little Italy** is next, along Preston Avenue and stretching south, and finally the **Wellington Street** area, which harbours plenty of good little eateries.

Chinatown

Scores of restaurants with enticing menus succeed each other along Somerset Street in Chinatown. **Yangtze** *($$; 700 Somerset St., ☎236-0555)* ranks among those establishments with solid reputations. Indeed, the place is always full to capacity. Its prodigious dining room is equipped with large round tables and thus is ideal for Sunday family dinners. Though somewhat impersonal, it is nonetheless pleasant. The menu features delectable Cantonese specialties.

Little Italy

Also in Little Italy, **Salvatore** *($$; 388 Booth St., ☎233-4731)* prepares good dishes in a quiet, gentle atmosphere, without the excessive decor typical of some Italian restaurants.

Ottawa West

At the beginning of Wellington Street, in its least inviting and most forgotten part, is hidden an exotic little pearl called **Addis Café** *($$; closed Mon; 1093 Wellington St., ☎725-5127)*. This is a real discovery. Solomon, the friendly owner, will guide you cheerfully through the wonders of Ethiopian cuisine, whose secret lies in combinations of different spices and seasonings. The setting is congenial, a small room with high ceilings and, on the walls, recent works of art that change every five or six weeks. The cooking will seduce you, especially if you like garlic, ginger and lentils. The base is a flat, pancake-shaped bread called *injera* on top of which other food is served. Small portions of this bread are used to scoop up the puréed lentils or the long-simmering meat stews. Solomon will be pleased to show you how to eat without utensils. Food can also be taken out. A must-taste!

Not far away, the **Won Ton House** *($$; 1300 Wellington St., ☎728-8885)* is a neighbourhood favourite, with Szechuanese and Cantonese dishes plus a few Indonesian items.

This little known part of town harbours a few boutiques and some good restaurants. Though the **Juniper** bistro *($$-$$$; 1293 Wellington St., ☎728-0220)* only recently opened its doors here, it soon left its mark. Its sparse decor, consisting merely of small, coloured frames and parchment lamps, turns out to be both soothing and elegant. The two perfectly lovely dining rooms are delightful; but what will catch your attention above all is the menu, featuring always toothsome and originally prepared dishes.

Almost next door, **Opus Bistro** *($$$; closed Sun and Mon; 1331 Wellington St., ☎722-9549)* is worth the trip. This small bistro, with dark, simple, tasteful decor, serves tasty and impeccably presented dishes, some of them marrying eclectic ingredients. Save room for the tempting desserts. The wine selection is enticing, by the glass or by the bottle, with some excellent South African, Australian or Californian wines at relatively inexpensive prices compared to better known vintages. Service is outstanding and friendly, with helpful advice on the best choices.

The Glebe

A number of boutiques with enticing window displays line Bank Street, near Glebe Street. These arrays are dazzling in the winter, especially in December, though you will have to dawdle along in order to truly contemplate them. Fortunately, you can then warm up and have something to eat at one of the pleasant **Starbucks**, **Guabbajabba** or **Second Cup** cafés located in the area. You will not be alone, however, for all three, with their selections of coffees and teas and mouthwatering goodies, are always full in the afternoons.

For excellent Indian dishes, make a reservation at the **New Delhi** *($$; 417 Bank St.,* ☎*237-4041)*. The friendly owner offers dishes prepared with fresh quality ingredients, and the food is never too spicy. The chicken tikka, a tandoori specialty, is absolutely delicious. There is a buffet for under $10, every day except Saturday. It is also possible to order take-out items by telephone or at the counter.

Fratelli *($$-$$$; 749 Bank St.,* ☎*237-1658)* is one of those restaurants one chances upon with delight. The sober decor, essentially composed of splendid hardwood floors, wall lights and a few mirrors, makes the place inviting at first glance. The menu, which features Italian dishes tastefully prepared in an innovative way, is equally attractive. A good place to keep in mind in the Glebe.

 HULL

A pleasant café/restaurant/bar/gallery/movie theatre/terrace with a very laid-back atmosphere, **Aux Quatre Jeudis** *($; 44 Rue Laval,* ☎*771-9557)* is patronized by a young, slightly bohemian clientele. It shows movies, and its pretty terrace is very popular in the summertime.

At **Pi-za'za** *($; 36 Rue Laval, ☎771-0565)*, you can sample an excellent variety of fine pizzas in a pleasant, relaxed atmosphere.

The **Cafe Laurier** *($-$$; 35 Rue Laurier)*, located in the lobby of the Ramada Plaza hotel, offers a good breakfast buffet, as well as a reasonably priced table d'hote in the evening. The laid-back atmosphere and courteous service make this a good place to keep in mind.

The **Fou du Roi** *($$; 253 Boulevard Saint-Joseph, ☎819-778-0516)* serves simple, consistently good food. It's a popular lunch spot and has a pleasant outdoor seating area during summer.

🏵 Le Twist *($$; 88 Rue Montcalm, ☎777-8886)* is known for its burgers, mussels and home-made fries, among the best in town, which are savoured in a charming setting and relaxed ambiance. In summer, a large, completely private terrace awaits you here. It is best to make reservations for lunch, as the place is often jam-packed.

A little restaurant specializing in French cuisine, **Le Panaché** *($$$; closed Sun and Mon; 201 Rue Eddy, ☎777-7771)* has a relaxed, intimate ambiance.

If you're looking for a good, unpretentious place to eat, head to **Le Pied Cochon** *($$$; closed Sun and Mon; 248 Montcalm, ☎777-5808)*, where the food is as varied as it is delicious, and the service is impeccable.

A former private house, **La Soupière** *($$$; closed Sun and Mon; 53 Kent, ☎771-6256)* offers excellent regional cuisine in large portions. As the restaurant is small, accommodating only 40 people, it is best to make reservations.

Le Tartuffe *($$$; closed Sun; 133 Rue Notre Dame, ☎776-6424)* is a marvelous little gourmet French restaurant located just steps from the Musée Canadien des Civilisations.

With its friendly, courteous service and delightful, intimate ambiance, this place is sure to win your heart.

Le Sans-Pareil *($$$-$$$$; closed Sun and Mon; 71 Boulevard St-Raymond, ☎771-1471)* is located 5 minutes from Hull's new casino, and right near the shopping centres. This is a Belgian restaurant, so it's only normal that chef Luc Gielen offers a two-for-one special on mussels (prepared in twelve different ways) on Tuesday nights. The sinfully good menu usually changes every three weeks, and the focus is on fresh products from various parts of Québec. The chef has a flair for combining ingredients in innovative ways, so don't hesitate to opt for the *menu gourmand*, which includes several courses, complete with the appropriate wines to wash them down. This place may be small, but it's truly charming. Check it out!

The Casino has all the facilities for your gambling pleasures – two restaurants serve excellent meals away from all the betting: **Banco** *($$)* offers a reasonably priced, quality buffet and various menu items; the more chic and expensive **Baccara** *($$$$; closed for lunch; 1 Boulevard du Casino, ☎772-6210)* has won itself a place among the best restaurants of the region. The set menu always consists of superb dishes that you can enjoy along with spectacular views of the lake. The well-stocked wine cellar and impeccable service round out this memorable culinary experience.

 The stylish **Café Henry Burger** *($$$$; 69 Laurier, ☎777-5646)* specializes in fine French cuisine. The menu changes according to the availability of the freshest ingredients, and always offers dishes to please the most discerning palate. The restaurant has long maintained an excellent reputation.

MERRICKVILLE

The dining room of the **Country Corner Tea Room** *($; Mill St.)* is very appealing with its antique furniture and pretty wallpaper with little blue geese. Everything is in place in this haven of tranquility. The menu offers simple, reasonably prices dishes like quiche.

The restaurant of the **Sam Jakes Inn** *($$$; 118 Main St. East,*
☎269-3711) offers an elaborate menu, with a choice between
beef dishes and fresh fish. These are savoured in the 19th-
century elegance of the inn's dining room.

ENTERTAINMENT

Ottawa has never been famous for its nightlife. Though its streets are often deserted after 11pm, you can top off your night enjoyably by knowing a few of its secrets. In addition to the warm pubs and lively bars, notably set up along Elgin Street and around Byward Market, the city has a flourishing cultural life. Excellent shows are presented at the National Arts Centre, where the city's various theatre companies perform. Finally, entertaining festivals are organized throughout the year.

 BARS AND NIGHTCLUBS

In the past, many Ontarians would finish off the night in Hull, for, until very recently, only the bars in that city were open until 3am. Since April 1996, however, the two cities have adopted the same closing hours, so that bars in both Ottawa and Hull now close at 2am. Whatever your preference, you will find enjoyable bars on either side of the Ottawa River.

Near downtown Ottawa, there are several bars and pubs along Elgin Street, which is quite lively in the evening.

Ottawa

Maxwell's *(340 Elgin St., ☎232-5771)*, upstairs from a restaurant, is popular with trendy youth. In the summer, there are tables on a large balcony facing the lively street.

Across the street is a very popular pub, **Lieutenant's Pump** *(361 Elgin St., ☎238-2949)*. There are a few tables outside in the summer, and food is available.

If you are put off by flashy bars, you may appreciate the youthful and unpretentious atmosphere of the **Fox and Feather** *(Elgin St., at MacLaren St.)*. A bar and large picture windows are all that decorate this noisy, smoky room, but the place boasts a fairly pleasant ambiance nonetheless.

Right next door, the **MacLaren** *(Elgin St., at MacLaren St.)* boasts a huge room in which several pool tables are set up. Those waiting for their turn can kill time by watching videos on the big-screen television.

Friday's Piano Bar *(150 Elgin St., ☎237-5353)* is more of a meeting spot for business people. It has an older clientele, some of whom end their evening here after dining at the restaurant of the same name.

The **D'Arcy McGee** pub *(44 Sparks St.)* can pride itself on being the only one in Ottawa to bear the title of real Irish pub, for the interior was completely built in Ireland, then transported to Ottawa where it was reconstructed piece by piece. Perfectly warm, fitted out with woodwork and stained-glass windows and decorated with scores of marvellous knick-knacks, the place is always full. Concerts are presented here on certain evenings. Good selection of beers on tap.

Yuk Yuk's *(Wed to Sat; 88 Albert St., ☎236-5233)* is part of a chain offering comedy shows, some of them actually quite funny. This is an interesting alternative to a conventional bar. No smoking on Thursdays.

The area around the Byward Market is home to several bars, many of them clustered along George and York streets.

Stoney's *(62 York St., ☎241-8858)* probably holds the record of longevity for disco-bars. It seems young people have been coming here forever to have a drink and dance on a small dance floor. In the summer, it is open in back. The music generally tends towards rock and roll.

Vineyard's Wine Bar Bistro *(54 York St., ☎241-4270)* is a friendly, congenial little bar where you can enjoy wine, beer and cheese. Musicians often perform here, with jazz at the top of the list.

Part of the well-known chain, Ottawa's **Hard Rock Café** *(73 York St.)* is a carbon copy of its sister establishments: blaring rock music and electric guitars adorning the walls.

If you prefer trendy nightclubs, opt for the **Theatre** *(Rideau St., at Dalhousie St.)* instead. A crowd eager to dance to rousing music is prepared to line up here on Saturday nights, until the doorman deigns to let them in. This "pick-up joint" also boasts a Cigar Lounge catering to budding stogie buffs.

Though lacking the character of the D'Arcy McGee, the **Heart and Crown** *(67 Clarence St.)* is another fashionable Irish pub in the capital. Relaxed ambiance and good selection of beers.

Ottawa just wouldn't be right whitout an English pub: so the **Earl of Sussex** *(431 Sussex Dr.)* was thus set up here. Warm decor, beer on tap and fish & chips on the menu as is only fitting in this type of establishment.

If the mere thought of spending hours in a smoky space where a mixed crowd jigs to the sounds of deafening music makes you shudder, opt for the chic **Zoe's** *(1 Rideau St.)*, at the Château Laurier. Everything here is calm and comfy; the place boasts delightfully soft music and cosy armchairs.

ENTERTAINMENT

Hull

For many years now, **Aux Quatre Jeudis** *(44 Laval)* has been *the* place for the café crowd. It has lots of ambiance, and there's a big, attractive terrace to hang out on in the summer.

Le Bop *(5 Aubry)* is a pleasant little place in old Hull. You can kick off your evening with a reasonably priced, decent meal. The music ranges from techno and disco to soft rock and even a little hard rock.

Le Fou du Roi *(253 Boulevard St-Joseph)* is where the thirty-something crowd hangs out. There's a dance floor, and the windows open onto a little terrace in the summertime. This place is also a popular after-work gathering place.

Gay Bar

Le Club *(77 Wellington St., ☎777-1411)* is a gay meeting spot that has been around for several years. Set on two stories, it has a crowded dance floor.

 THEATRES

The **National Arts Centre** *(53 Elgin St., ☎996-5051, ☞996-9578)* is Ottawa's cultural headquarters, with an opera house and two theatres where top-notch performances are offered year-round.

Ottawa has several theatre companies in addition to those staging their plays at the National Arts Centre.

The **Great Canadian Theatre Company** *(910 Gladstone Ave., ☎236-5196)* presents plays by Canadian dramaturges.

The **Ottawa Little Theatre** *(400 King Edward Ave., ☎233-8948)* is a community theatre company that often stages interesting plays.

The **Odyssey Theatre** is distinctive in that it specializes in outdoor plays. During the summer, the company performs in Strathcona Park *($18; 2 Daly Ave., ☎232-8407)*.

Finally, Ottawa also boasts an opera house, the **Opera Lyra Ottawa** *(110 Daly Ave., ☎232-9200)*.

Movie Theatres

Cineplex Odeon: World Exchange Plaza, 111 Albert Street.

Somerset: 386 Somerset Street West.

Famous Players: Capital Square, 230 Queen Street.

Rideau Centre: 50 Rideau Street.

Bytowne (repertory cinema): 325 Rideau Street.

CASINO

Those looking to have fun while standing a good chance of winning a fair amount of money can head to the **Casino de Hull** *(11pm to 3am; 1 Boulevard du Casino, ☎819-772-2100 or 1-800-665-2274)*. The vast casino notably comprises slot machines, Keno, blackjack and roulette tables, as well as two restaurants (see p 132).

 FESTIVALS AND CULTURAL EVENTS

Febuary

Winterlude no longer needs an introduction: its reputation is well established in Canada. It consists of 10 days of winter festivities of all sorts in early February and is centred on what is billed as the world's longest skating rink.

May

The **Tulip Festival** is held in May, during the Victoria Day long weekend. The city is then decked with thousands of tulips, bestowed by the Netherlands by way of thanks to Canada for taking in Queen Wilhemina during the Second World War.

ENTERTAINMENT

Shows and activities of all kinds in various parts of the city, including Confederation Park and Dow's Lake.

June

The **Festival Franco-Ontarien** is held at the end of June. This is a celebration of French culture in Ontario. There are activities of all sorts, handicrafts stalls, and an important series of shows presenting many of the greats of French song from here and elsewhere.

July

The **Festival Canada** (☎996-5051) takes place in July. Culture holds pride of place for four weeks as 70 dance, jazz and opera performances are presented at the National Arts Centre.

In early July, the blues take over as the nation's capital welcomes a few of the biggest names in blues for the three days of the **Ottawa Blues Festival** (☎233-8798). Concerts take place at Confederation Park.

In the last two weeks of July, jazz enthusiasts get their turn enjoying themselves to the fullest while the **Ottawa International Jazz Festival** (☎594-3580, www.jazz.ottawa.com) is in full swing. Concerts at Confederation Park.

During **Gay Pride** week, in mid-July, a host of activities (parade, picnic and shows) take place in order to celebrate the city's gay and lesbian community.

August

The casino's opening was the origin of an annual fireworks festival, **Les Grands Feux du Casino** (☎819-771-FEUX or 1-800-771-FEUX), held every year during the month of August.

SPECTATOR SPORTS

Ottawa has had its own National Hockey League (NHL) team, the **Senators** *(1000 Palladium Dr., ☎771-7367 or 1-800-444-7367, ⇒599-0358, www.ottawasenators.com)*, since 1992. Those who wish to attend one of the games played at the Corel Centre must drive there, because it is located in Kanata, a dozen kilometres from town. To get there by car, take the 417 heading west and turn off at Palladium Drive, which leads straight to the arena. If you prefer public transportation, take a bus at one of the Transitway stations, then transfer to one of the stops with the Corel Centre logo (buses 401, 402, 403, 404 and 405 all stop at the centre).

The **Ottawa Lynx** *(300 Coventry Rd., ☎747-5969 or 1-800-663-0985, ⇒747-0003, www.magi.com/lynx/)*, the local baseball team, is a subsidiary of the National Baseball League's Montreal Expos. Those attending the games played by the Lynx will be treated to a match of excellent calibre as this is the ultimate grade before the major leagues.

ENTERTAINMENT

SHOPPING

Ottawa has plenty to offer those who consider prowling along main thoroughfares bordered by enticing shop windows among the pleasures of travelling. Indeed, the city boasts four areas ideal for abandoning yourselves entirely to shopping: Sparks Street, Bank Street, Elgin Street and the area surrounding Byward Market. In summer, Byward Market, with its flower, fruit and vegetable vendors, is unquestionably the liveliest. During the holiday season, Bank Street has a unique cachet as the city is festooned with an abundance of lights. One thing is sure, whatever the time of year, you will be able to unearth a thousand and one finds as you walk the streets of the capital.

 UPPER TOWN

Sparks Street, a long pedestrianized thouroughfare lined with trees, benches and lovely shops, makes for a very pleasant little stroll. On rainy days, when walking the streets proves less appealing, you can opt for a stop at the **240 Sparks** shopping centre, which comprises several attractive boutiques. Among these is **Holt Renfrew**, which offers a wide choice of high-quality items, including men and women's clothing by great European, American and Canadian designers, beauty products and accessories.

For very classical, well-cut garments for both women and men, a stop at Marks and Spencer *(194 Sparks St.)* is a must. The shop has acquired a loyal clientele as it also boasts a grocery section rife with an endless variety of biscuits, chocolates and other delicacies.

Kitchen Supplies

Showing great wariness is necessary upon entering the rather cluttered McIntosh & Watts boutique *(193 Sparks St.)*, where crystal vases and glasses, china, candelabras and knick-knacks of all kinds vie for space here and there in somewhat precarious fashion. Caution is all the more necessary as certain very beautiful items are quite expensive. You will not fail, however, to unearth something here with which to beautify your home.

Handicrafts

Sparks Street, between Elgin and O'Connor Streets, is a good place to shop for Canadian-made handicrafts. The first among many such shops is the Snow Goose *(83 Sparks St.)*, which boasts a wide selection of creations by Inuit and Native-American artisans, including sculptures and engravings. The shop also carries an abundance of leather and fur accoutrements, notably mocassins, gloves and hats.

A stone's throw away, Canada's Four Corners *(93 Sparks St.)* also sells Native-American handicrafts; however, finding a good-quality item requires rummaging and sorting through the assorted junk and plastic objects. Plastic place mats, T-shirts bearing Canada's colours, Inuit sculptures and leather mocassins are all jumbled together here. At the very back of the store are reproductions of engravings by native artists (Norval Morisseau, Benjamin Chee-Chee, Doris Cyrette, etc.), perhaps the greatest find in the place.

Music

Looking to purchase a CD of some kind? Then head to **HMV** *(211 Sparks St.)*, the well-known chain specializing in recordings of all musical genres, where you are sure to find it.

Office Supplies

Grand & Toy *(116 Albert St.)* is hardly a place worth rushing to, but it is a useful one if you are looking for envelopes, paper, notebooks, pencils, or any office supplies you may be short of during your stay.

Books

Canada Books *(Sparks St.)* has a fine selection of Canadian books, whether it be literature, arts, photography or other topics.

If your visit to Canada Books has proven fruitless, you can check out the incredible selection at the **Smithbooks** shop, across the street. In addition to a wide choice of works about Canada, the place carries books dealing with various subjects, as well as novels, beautiful tomes and travel guidebooks.

For newspapers, books and magazines from all over, try the **Place Bell Books** *(175 Metcalfe St., ☎233-3821)* or the **Maison de la Presse Internationale** *(100 Bank St., ☎230-9774)*.

Stamps and Antique Prints

Upon entering the small, cluttered **Ian Kimmerly Stamps** shop *(112 Sparks St.)*, you will have the impression of having gone back in time, for antique prints, often over 100 years old, take up every inch of space. The place also has a small section devoted to stamps, mainly patronized by collectors who come to spend hours indulging their passion: searching through mountains of little stamps for the most valuable one.

SHOPPING

LOWER TOWN

A shopping mall par excellence in the capital, the Rideau Centre *(50 Rideau St.)*, with some 200 shops including Eaton, is unquestionably the place to find anything and everything. Noteworthy among this succession of stores of all kinds are HMV (music store), the Disney store, Oh Yes Ottawa (for souvenirs of the city), Mrs. Tiggy Winkles (toys), The Gap (clothing for all) and Roots (leather garments). The centre also houses two pharmacies, banks (Royal, Nova Scotia, TD), as well as several fast-food restaurants and Marché Mövenpick (see p 123).

For window shopping and some interesting finds, nothing beats a stroll around the Byward Market. Winter or summer, the central pavillion, where vegetable dealers gather in the summer, houses a multitude of handicraft stalls on two floors. You can buy all sorts of items: jewellery, leather goods, scarves, paintings, and so on. The vegetable market lies at the heart of the action in the summer. It is a pleasant spot to shop or merely to linger.

Kitchen Supplies

Domus is not only the name of a very good restaurant (see p 128), but also the name of a top-of-the-line kitchenware store. Domus Housewares *(85 Murray St., ☎241-6410)* is vast and bright. Besides selling almost every kitchen accessory imaginable, it offers cookbooks for every taste, from which the recipes for dishes prepared at the restaurant are drawn.

Garden Supplies

A little further along the street, another Domus shop, this time Domus Gardens *(101 Murray St., ☎562-3275)* offers exquisite pots, vases and garden accessories.

Sporting Goods

Backpacks, top-quality camping material at good prices, and sports clothes are part of the assortment you will find at **Mountain Equipment Co-op** *(5B Beechwood St., ☎745-1094)*. This is the place to go to equip yourself for an outdoor excursion.

Handicrafts

The **OXFAM** boutique *(495 Sussex Dr.)* is the just the place in the capital to find gratification while contributing to a good cause. The shop sells a host of hand-crafted objects from all over the world, and profits help finance the humanitarian organization.

Jewellery

Those who appreciate unusual jewels should pop round to **Striking** *(531A Sussex Dr.)*, whose gold or silver earrings, necklaces, brooches and bracelets are sure to prove irresistible.

Home Decoration

Whether you are looking for lamps, candelabras, mirrors, dishes or furniture, dropping by **Côte Sud** *(Sussex Dr.)* is sure to give you lots of original ideas for beautifying your home. Indeed, the hardest thing about visiting this shop will be resisting its many temptations.

If you have left Côte Sud unscathed or, rather less likely, without having found exactly what you wanted, head to the **Zone** boutique *(471 Sussex Dr.)*, located a short distance away, which offers an equally enticing selection of interior decor objects.

Folio *(459 Sussex Dr., ☎241-6336)* is another good place for home decoration, particularly for those ready to make

SHOPPING

extravagant purchases such as a Kosta Boda vase or an Alesi item.

Those who consider buying Christmas decorations in the middle of July to be perfectly normal will be delighted with the Christmas & Candles shop *(481 Sussex Dr., ☎241-5476)*, which overflows with tree decorations and ornaments of all kinds year-round.

The Lynda Greenberg gallery *(13 Murray St., ☎241-2767)* will mainly appeal to those who like to adorn their homes with vases and tasteful knick-knacks whose shapes and colours are both original and refined. Nothing very classical, only small masterpieces of distinction.

By continuing your stroll to Elgin Street, you will come across another row of shops with inviting window displays. Indeed, the Art & Home's shop window will hardly leave you indifferent, heralding, and rightly so, a great many attractive household items (extra furniture, vases, etc.).

Food

Bagel Bagel *(92 Clarence St., ☎241-8998)* is an establishment that prepares bagels in 1,001 ways. The countless varieties of bagels produced here are sold at the counter. Something for every taste.

Close by, the Valley Goods Company *(41 York St., ☎241-3000)* offers various products in the tradition of an old-fashioned general store. You can buy chocolate, jams, chutneys, ice cream, original greeting cards, and an array of other items.

Vintages *(299 Dalhousie St., ☎562-9403)* is the specialty store of the Liquor Control Board of Ontario. There are frequent wine tastings (for a fee).

Gift Ideas

The museum shop at the National Gallery of Canada *(380 Sussex Dr.)* is just the place for those who like to rummage for hours through a mind-boggling amount of reproductions, be they posters, jewellery or decorative objects. In addition to these quality copies, the boutique boasts an amazing collection of art books as well as works by Native-American and Canadian artisans and sculptors.

Fans of Tintin or Asterix should pop round to **Planet BD** *(493 Sussex Dr., ☎789-6307)*, where several figurines and effigies of these comic-book heroes are displayed. The cost of some of these items may seem exorbitant, but, after having admired the finely detailed hand-made objects, you will compare them to small works of art rather than mere paraphernalia.

Finding the appropriate words to describe **Cow's** *(43 Clarence St., ☎789-COWS)* can prove rather difficult. The shop notably carries T-shirts and other cotton apparel, coffee mugs and other kitchen items, all adorned with stylized cows and short, amusing captions. Delicious ice-cream is also served here.

Books, Newspapers and Magazines

Part of the huge chain of bookshops, Ottawa's **Chapters** *(Rideau St., at Sussex Dr.)* boasts an incredible selection of books for all tastes, in both English and French.

There is really only one place to procure French books in the nation's capital: **Librairie du Soleil** *(321 Dalhousie St., ☎241-6999)*.

Coins

Numismatists should not fail to visit the shop at the **royal Canadian Mint** *(320 Sussex Dr.)*, in the very building where collectable Canadian coins are minted. The very latest creations, in silver, gold and platinum, are displayed here for sale.

SHOPPING

Beauty Products

The displays are so lovely and the products smell so good at the Belle de Provence boutique *(Georges St., at Dalhousie St.)*, you will have the uncontrollable urge to buy everything in sight. Mild soaps for softer skin, natural shampoos... enough to make you indulge in a spending spree!

 THE GLEBE

In fine weather, you may leave Sparks Street and explore Bank Street, another one of Ottawa's pleasant main thoroughfares. As you walk along, the street becomes alternately dull and seductive, but it will not fail to charm you. It boasts two distinct commercial sections: one around Somerset Street and a second one south of Queensway.

Kitchen Supplies

No one should purchase any kitchen article whatsoever without having first compared its price at the Great Glebe Emporium. The shelves here are jam-packed with plates, glasses, bowls, saucepans (notably Paderno brand) and frying pans, always sold at discount prices. In places, extricating the coveted item from the shelf without knocking anything down can seem a daunting task. Another piece of advice before entering: summon up your patience, for the aisles are narrow and the shop is always crowded.

Right next door, J. D. Adam *(795 Bank St., ☎235-8714)* harbours fewer low-priced treasures, but still contains a good selection of quality items as well as various decorative objects.

Home Decoration

The Orient has always inspired dreaming. By popping over to the East Wind boutique *(794 Bank St., ☎567-0382)*, you may succeed in finding some treasure that evokes these distant lands.

Gift Ideas

The **Unicef** boutique *(379 Bank St.)* boasts many hand-crafted works from different parts of the world.

Nature takes pride of place at **Humback** *(775 Bank St., ☎235-5792)*, where books, pins, photographs and knick-knacks all touch on flora and fauna.

Toys

The very beautiful high-quality toys at **Mrs. Tiggy Winkles** *(809 Bank St., ☎234-3836)* have been delighting children since time immemorial.

Art Supplies

Paintbrushes, pencils, sketch pads... Two good places to know about in the capital are **Wallack's** and **Omer Deserres**, both on Bank Street.

Stationery

The Papery *(11A William St., ☎241-1212)* is the top spot for paper supplies: magnificent greeting cards, agendas, calendars, wrapping paper, filing boxes in various sizes, and so forth. There is another branch in the Glebe *(850 Bank St., ☎230-1313)*.

Clothing

At **La Cache**, you are sure to find a little something to please you *(763 Bank St.)*, for the boutique overflows with a profusion of goods: cotton and wool garments, scarves and hats of all kinds, beauty products, bedding, knick-knacks and dishes.

For leather bags, shoes and coats, both casual and durable, head to **Roots** *(787 Bank St.)*, whose reputation is long-standing. Other items, such as wool sweaters, are also worth the trip.

Piles and piles and sweaters in every colour of the rainbow clutter the walls of **Penelope's Haberdashery** *(81 Bank St., ☎232-9565)*. Finding something here therefore entails taking the time to rummage through the countless, often classically cut, but always high-quality wool sweaters.

HULL

The **boutique of the Musée Canadien des Civilizations** *(100 Rue Laurier)* is, in a way, part of the exhibit. Although the Canadian and native craft pieces aren't of the same quality as those exhibited at the museum, you'll find all sorts of reasonably priced treasures and lots of great little curios.

The museum also has a **bookstore** with a wonderful collection on the history of crafts in many different cultures.

MERRICKVILLE

Mirick's Landing *(St. Lawrence St.)* sells a fine variety of items, including soaps, candles, tablecloths and napkins, and various trinkets.

The enticing selection of candies, fruit preserves, vinegars and other irresistible products at **Mrs. McGarrigle's** *(St. Lawrence St.)* is enough to make your mouth water.

INDEX

■ ULYSSES TRAVEL GUIDES

☐ Affordable B&Bs
   in Québec . . . . . $12.95 CAN
                $9.95 US
☐ Atlantic Canada $24.95 CAN
               $17.95 US
☐ Beaches of Maine $12.95 CAN
                $9.95 US
☐ Bahamas . . . . . $24.95 CAN
               $17.95 US
☐ Calgary . . . . . . $17.95 CAN
               $12.95 US
☐ Canada . . . . . . $29.95 CAN
               $21.95 US
☐ Chicago . . . . . . $19.95 CAN
               $14.95 US
☐ Chile . . . . $27.95 CAN
               $17.95 US
☐ Costa Rica . . . . $27.95 CAN
               $19.95 US
☐ Cuba . . . . $24.95 CAN
               $17.95 US
☐ Dominican
   Republic . . . . . . $24.95 CAN
               $17.95 US
☐ Ecuador Galapagos
   Islands . . . . $24.95 CAN
               $17.95 US
☐ El Salvador . . . . $22.95 CAN
               $14.95 US
☐ Guadeloupe . . . $24.95 CAN
               $17.95 US
☐ Guatemala . . . . $24.95 CAN
               $17.95 US
☐ Honduras . . . . . $24.95 CAN
               $17.95 US
☐ Jamaica . . . . . . $24.95 CAN
               $17.95 US
☐ Lisbon . . . . $18.95 CAN
               $13.95 US
☐ Louisiana . . . . . $29.95 CAN
               $21.95 US
☐ Martinique . . . . $24.95 CAN
               $17.95 US
☐ Montréal . . . . . $19.95 CAN
               $14.95 US
☐ New Orleans . . $17.95 CAN
               $12.95 US

☐ New York City . $19.95 CAN
               $14.95 US
☐ Nicaragua . . . . $24.95 CAN
               $16.95 US
☐ Ontario . . . . . . $24.95 CAN
               $14.95US
☐ Ottawa . . . . . . $17.95 CAN
               $12.95 US
☐ Panamá . . . . . . $24.95 CAN
               $16.95 US
☐ Portugal . . . . . . $24.95 CAN
               $16.95 US
☐ Provence - Côte
   d'Azur . . . . $29.95 CAN
               $21.95US
☐ Québec . . . . . . $29.95 CAN
               $21.95 US
☐ Québec and Ontario
   with Via . . . . $9.95 CAN
               $7.95 US
☐ Toronto . . . . . . $18.95 CAN
               $13.95 US
☐ Vancouver . . . . $17.95 CAN
               $12.95 US
☐ Washington D.C. $18.95 CAN
               $13.95 US
☐ Western Canada $29.95 CAN
               $21.95 US

■ ULYSSES DUE SOUTH

☐ Acapulco . . . . . $14.95 CAN
               $9.95 US
☐ Belize . . . . $16.95 CAN
               $12.95 US
☐ Cartagena
   (Colombia) . . . . $12.95 CAN
               $9.95 US
☐ Cancun Cozumel $17.95 CAN
               $12.95 US
☐ Puerto Vallarta . $14.95 CAN
               $9.95 US
☐ St. Martin and
   St. Barts . . . . . $16.95 CAN
               $12.95 US

■ ULYSSES GREEN ESCAPES

☐ Cycling in France $22.95 CAN
$16.95 US
☐ Hiking in the Northeastern
United States .. $19.95 CAN
$13.95 US
☐ Hiking in Québec $19.95 CAN
$13.95 US

■ ULYSSES TRAVEL JOURNAL

☐ Ulysses Travel Journal
(Blue, Red, Green,
Yellow, Sextant) . $9.95 CAN
$7.95 US

QUANTITY	TITLES	PRICE	TOTAL

NAME:_____   Sub-total
ADDRESS:_____   Postage & Handling $8.00*
_____   Sub-total
Payment: ☐ Money Order ☐ Visa ☐   G.S.T.in Canada 7%
Card   TOTAL
Signature:_____

ULYSSES TRAVEL PUBLICATIONS
4176 St-Denis, Montréal, QC, H2W
2M5
(514) 843-9447 fax (514) 843-
9448
www.ulysses.ca
*$15 for overseas orders

U.S. ORDERS: **GLOBE PEQUOT PRESS**
P.O. Box 833, 6 Business Park Road,
Old Saybrook, CT 06475-0833
1-800-243-0495 fax 1-800-820-
2329
www.globe-pequot.com